Ship-Specific Guides

Volume 2: Autonomous Surface Ships

To

The Futurists

Of Our Global Maritime Industry

Ship-Specific Guides

Volume 2: Autonomous Surface Ships

Elstan A. Fernandez

SHROFF PUBLISHERS & DISTRIBUTORS PVT. LTD.
Mumbai *Bangalore* *Kolkata* *New Delhi*

Ship-Specific Guides
Volume 2: Autonomous Surface Ships

By *Elstan A. Fernandez*

First Edition: March 2024

Print ISBN: 978-93-5542-678-9

E_Book ISBN: 978-93-5542-808-0

Published by **Shroff Publishers and Distributors Pvt. Ltd.** B-103, Railway Commercial Complex, Sector 3, Sanpada (E), Navi Mumbai 400705
TEL: (91 22) 4158 4158 • FAX: (91 22) 4158 4141
E-mail : spdorders@shroffpublishers.com • Web : www.shroffpublishers.com
Printed at SAP Print Solutions Pvt. Ltd., Mumbai

Preface to the First Edition

This compiled pocketbook is based on recent research of autonomous ships and from my experience in the field of automation, control, and remote monitoring of both local and remotely located equipment and vast systems on UMS ships and the older versions too. It is intended to be a primer for the autonomous ships that will evolve over the next decade. Large, world-famous, and well-established organisations expect to roll-out ocean-going, unmanned cargo ships by 2035.

Control systems have evolved from crude mechanical computers to vacuum tube-based ones to relays for logic gates, followed by semiconductors and finally what the world sees today – an explosion of technologies!

Similarly, maritime communication began with semaphore flags, went on to flashing lights for night-time communication, to Morse code and now there is a host of electronic communication systems that have flooded the market, vying for their own space and bandwidth!

The next decade will be a game-changer for the shipping industry as it is one of the last to benefit from tried and tested remote, unmanned operations to operate in the merciless seas, under unpredictable weather conditions, and to top it all, piracy too! Manning of ships will reduce over the next decade, but new avenues will open up ashore for those who can adapt to these evolving technologies.

The IMO is playing a significant role as always in ensuring that every aspect of safety is adhered to and also the designation of the right people in the right place where operations is considered. Hence, relevant, and current IMO guidelines for Maritime Autonomous Surface Ships have also been included. Seafarers who are currently engaged with commercial ships and those undergoing training to qualify for these positions, will find this book useful.

The Pocketbook Series was introduced because there is a changing trend in the way books are read today. The new normal is that readers and students prefer to read specific, and not so voluminous content, in the least time, as time comes at a premium these days.

Hopefully our team of authors will be able to cater to numerous topics from many relevant subjects.

Any feedback is always welcome!

Elstan A. Fernandez

Acknowledgement

The opportunity to share my acquired knowledge with thousands of professionals and students across many countries and organisations has given me an immense sense of accomplishment and satisfaction. It has also been a wonderful journey of discovery for me - both while researching for this book and teaching the subject in India and abroad.

This compiled book is the result of almost 45 years of learning and hands-on experience in this field, including over 25 years of research and collaboration with various organisations and specialists in the global maritime industry.

I sincerely thank all the wonderful people who have supported me in every way, ever since I embarked on this journey as an author.

I am indebted to many distinguished persons who have have not only supported my endeavours but also permitted me to publish very valuable content for education. These articles are relevant to the building, safe operation, and conscientious survey of commercial ships. Many world-class organisations and manufacturers have extended their invaluable support too. I am grateful for the updated information from their websites and related literature. These inclusions have undoubtedly enriched the content.

Numerous students now realize their dream of being educated through a scholarship program that is funded by the royalty that I receive.

The encouragement from lay people and professionals alike has thus been a stimulus to my enthusiasm. To give back and say "thank you" to the maritime fraternity, I also host a free educational website – www.marineelectricity.com.

In this context, I have a beautiful quote to share with my readers:

"Real knowledge, like everything else of value, is not to be obtained easily.

It must be worked for, studied for, thought for, and, more than all must be prayed for."

Thomas Arnold (1795-1842), British Educator, Scholar

Contents

Contents

Chapter 1

Guidelines

1.1 Introduction to Autonomous Surface Ships

A ship's ability to monitor its own health, establish and communicate what is around it and make decisions based on that information is vital to the development of autonomous operations. The need is to develop a set of electronic senses that inform an electronic brain and allow the vessel to navigate safely and avoid collisions.

1.1.1 Sensor Fusion

Sensor technology is well developed and found in many forms of autonomous vehicles, most notably cars, where competing developers have prioritised differing technologies.

Many projects have explored the contribution that different sensor technologies make in providing a vessel or its remote operators with an accurate perspective of the vessel's surroundings at all times and in all conditions. Looking at different types of radars, high-definition visual cameras, thermal imaging, and LIDAR, it has been concluded that fusing multiple sensor inputs provide the best results (Lidar, which stands for Light Detection and Ranging, is a remote sensing method that uses light in the form of a pulsed laser to measure ranges to the Earth).

The main question is not can this be done? It is how do we combine these technologies in the most cost-effective way considering the challenges of the maritime environment. Finding the optimum way to combine the different sensor technologies in a range of operating and climatic conditions is based on a series of tests at sea. It is now used in self-driven cars for the automatic driving assistance system ADAS).

1.1.2 Control Algorithms

Navigation and collision avoidance will be particularly important for remotely controlled and autonomous ships, allowing them to decide what action to take in the light of the sensory information received.

The decision algorithms behind this need perfecting, as it requires an interpretation of maritime rules and regulations. This leads to interpretation challenges for the programmer.

The development of control algorithms for autonomous vessels will be a gradual, iterative process and subject to extensive testing and simulation.

1.1.3 Communication and Connectivity

Autonomous vessels will still need human input from land, making connectivity between the ship and the crew crucial. Such communication will need to be bi-directional, accurate, scalable, and supported by multiple systems – creating redundancy and minimising risk. Sufficient communication link capacity for monitoring of the ship's sensors and remote control, when necessary, has to be guaranteed.

Manufacturers are finding ways to combine existing communication technologies in an optimum way for autonomous ship control.

They have created a simulated autonomous ship control system which will be connected to a satellite communications link as well as land-based systems. This will allow them to explore the behaviour of the complete system.

The operation of remote and autonomous ships will need to be at least as safe as existing vessels if they are to secure regulatory approval, the support of ship owners, operators, seafarers, and wider public acceptance.

Remote and autonomous ships have the potential to reduce human-based errors, but at the same time may modify some existing risks as well as create new types of risk. These circumstances and possible remedies will need to be explored. The marine industry has some experience on systematic and comprehensive risk assessments.

However, when new, emerging technology is involved, new knowledge, wider and deeper understanding of new and changed risk (with a variety of known and unknown hazards) is needed; guided by research it will lead us to new approaches.

Cybersecurity will be critical to the safe and successful operation of remote and autonomous vessels. We must identify and adapt the current best practices from a range of industries for application in the marine environment. The results will be used to make recommendations to regulators and to classification societies and other partners to support development work for creating the first set of standards for remote and unmanned vessel operation.

We know by now that a vessel's voyage is covered by a range of national, international, and private legal frameworks. To further complicate matters, maritime law does not anticipate the development of remote or autonomous ships. This presents many ambiguities. For example, does a ship's master or crew necessarily have to be on board the ship?

For remote controlled and autonomous shipping to become a reality we need efforts at all regulatory levels. The legal challenges of constructing and operating a demonstration vessel at a national level need to be explored, while simultaneously considering appropriate rule changes at the IMO.

Questions of liability for autonomous ships are subject to national variations, but generally it seems that there is less need for regulatory change in the field. What needs to be explored, however, is to what extent other liability rules, such as product liability, would affect traditional rules of maritime liability and insurance in the field of autonomous shipping.

Legislation can be changed if there is a political will. Teams plan to continue researching this element of the law, and to propose solutions, throughout various programs.

In the end, however, the necessary regulatory actions at national and international levels need to be taken by governments.

The industry wants to work with IMO to make sure the developing regulations are goal-based, safe and realistic.

Since the advent of shipping, seafarers have been integrally involved in ship operations, appropriate manning is considered an essential element of the seaworthiness of a ship and a prerequisite to ensure authorization to operate in national and international waters.

The outsourcing of some activities to mechanical counterparts and the lack of crew requires the re-thinking of several legal obligations undertaken by the flag states to certify the function of a vessel and could alter the liability regimes in which commercial ships operate. For example:

- Would automated ships with no crew on board be considered as sea-going vessels under UNCLOS, international and national law?
- How would minimum manning requirements for various tasks onboard the ship (such as watchkeeping, anchoring, loading and discharge) have to evolve to consider extensive automation?

- How would training of the existing crew develop to familiarize the crew with new digital tools?
- Could automated systems react in exceptional situations requiring situational judgement such as decision-making to avoid collisions / respond to pollution incidents and deviations to save human life at sea?
- Would remote operators based at the shore be considered seafarers?
- Could manufacturers of a device / faulty component of an automation system be liable for the damages caused due to a malfunction? Would they be covered by a limitation of liability regime?

Other questions arising are whether all national jurisdictions would allow the operation of Maritime Autonomous Surface Ships in their waters and, importantly, how saving life and property at sea can be ensured in practice, in the absence of any crew on board.

These questions are of significant importance, including for developing States, which account for over 80% of flag states and are among the major seafarer- supplying jurisdictions.

A harmonization of the legal framework surrounding the subject (through either soft law or binding legal instruments) would both increase the safety of navigation and facilitate trade.

As highlighted in UNCTAD's Review of Maritime Transport 2019, it would also ensure that seafarers originating from developing states are re-skilled in accordance with the more recent needs and requirements of an automated reality on board of MASS, as automation could render some tasks onboard obsolete.

1.2 IMO Scoping Exercise for the use of MASS

In response to the numerous questions arising on the subject and to ensure that regulation remains pertinent in the light of technological developments, the IMO initiated in 2017, a regulatory scoping exercise for the use of maritime autonomous surface ships (MASS) by the Maritime Safety Committee (MSC), as well as the Legal (LEG) and Facilitation (FAL) Committees, which was concluded in 2021.

The goal of the scoping exercise was to assess existing IMO instruments to see how they would apply to ships with varying degrees of automation.

The MSC, in June 2021 in the outcomes of the regulatory exercise, concluded that some high priority issues would need to be addressed in respect of several maritime conventions focusing on the safety of navigation, such as the International Convention for the Safety of Life at Sea 1974 (SOLAS) as amended; the International Convention on Standards of Training, Certification and Watchkeeping for Seafarers, 1978 (STWC) as amended; the International Convention for the Prevention of Pollution from Ships, 1973-1978 (MARPOL) as amended; and the Convention on the International Regulations for Preventing Collisions at Sea 1972 (COLREGs).

Those included:

The development of MASS terminology and definitions for the meaning of the terms ''MASS'', "master", "crew" or "responsible person", particularly in Degrees Three (remotely controlled ship) and Four (fully autonomous ship).

The functional and operational requirements of the remote-control station / center and the possible designation of a remote operator as seafarer.

The revision of provisions relating to manual operations and alarms on the bridge and other actions by the personnel (such as firefighting, cargoes stowage and securing and maintenance); watchkeeping; implications for search and rescue; and information required to be on board for safe operation.

• The LEG, in December 2021, on the other hand arrived at the conclusion that the existing provisions of the international conventions under its purview (such as for example the International Convention on Civil Liability for Oil Pollution Damage 1969 and its 1992 Protocol, the International Convention on the Establishment of an International Fund for Compensation for Oil Pollution Damage 1971 and its 1992 Protocol (FUND), the International Convention on Civil Liability for Bunker Oil Pollution Damage 2001 (BUNKER), the International Convention on Salvage 1989) could accommodate the concept of MASS, although in some cases interpretations or amendments might be required. These include:

• The role and the responsibility of the master / remote operator and especially the division of tasks between them.

• Questions of liability, and notions such as negligence / fault / recklessness might not be applicable, issues of causation might be more difficult to prove, while the determination personal fault of the shipowner / carrier and vicarious liability / third party liability would have to be re-thought under the prism of national law.

• Certification required under the conventions might have to be reconsidered, especially in Degrees Three and Four where there is no seafarer onboard.

The LEG also highlighted that conventions that are not under the auspices of the IMO, such as UNCLOS and the MLC 2006, might have to consider any future work of the IMO on MASS.

Finally, the FAL Committee, which supervises the implementation of the Convention on Facilitation of International Maritime Traffic agreed with most of the conclusions of the MSC and LEG relating to the need for definitions and clarifications of certain terms in the context of the FAL Convention. It highlighted that consideration should be given to situations such as the discovery of stowaways and the accommodation of people rescued at sea and refugees. It also emphasized that effective information exchange with the introduction of MASS might require machine-readable and decentralized format based on open and interoperable interfaces to enable automated processes.

1.2.1 The Way Forward

With the finalization of the scoping exercise, and after the agreement of all three engaged committees, in April 2022, MSC 105 designed a roadmap to develop a non-mandatory goal-based MASS Code with a view to adoption in the second half of 2024. Based on the experience gained in its application, a mandatory MASS Code might follow, which would enter into force on 1 January 2028. The IMO also organized, in September 2022 an online Seminar on Development of a Regulatory Framework for MASS with broad participation of researchers, academia, the private sector and IMO Member States to explore the subject and facilitate the lifting of certain regulatory obstacles.

In addition to the above, a Joint MSC-LEG-FAL Working Group was established as a cross-cutting mechanism to address common high-priority issues identified by the regulatory scoping exercises conducted by the three committees. To date, the first session the MSC-LEG-FAL Joint Working Group that took place on September 2022 considered issues perceived as high priority by all three Committees, namely:

- The definition of the term "master", its role, and responsibilities. The role and competences of the crew of a MASS (and its potential designation of its status as seafarer).
- The definition of "remote control station/center" and its requirements
- The definition of the term "remote operator", its responsibilities, required competencies and status as a seafarer.

No decisions were reached in the group, but a template was created for the participating Member States to identify and collect information of options for interpretations in view of the next meeting, which is scheduled to take place sometime in 2023 according to the approved roadmap. It was also agreed by the Joint Working Group to organize another seminar, this time on legal issues including UNCLOS, back-to-back with the next MASS-JWG meeting. Thus, important work on the legal framework to accommodate MASS is ongoing at the IMO. The outcome would hopefully provide for much-needed legal certainty in matters related to the safe and secure operation of automated vessels and would undeniably spur more legislative change both in other international fora as well as at national levels. Developing countries and seafarers' associations should take advantage of the opportunity to have their voice heard at this key juncture and consider becoming actively involved in this important ongoing work.

The IMO wants to ensure that the regulatory framework for Maritime Autonomous Surface Ships (MASS) keeps pace with technological developments that are rapidly evolving.

The IMO has recently completed a regulatory scoping exercise on Maritime Autonomous Surface Ships (MASS) that was designed to assess existing IMO instruments to see how they might apply to ships with varying degrees of automation. The regulatory scoping exercise (RSE) for safety treaties was finalized at the 103rd Session of the MSC in May 2021. Thus, important work on the legal framework to accommodate MASS is ongoing at the IMO. The outcome would hopefully provide for much-needed legal certainty in matters related to the safe and secure operation of automated vessels and would undeniably spur more legislative change both in other international fora as well as at national levels. Developing countries and seafarers' associations should take advantage of the opportunity to have their voice heard at this key juncture and consider becoming actively involved in this important ongoing work.

A transition to remote-controlled and autonomous vessels will also have an impact on shipping, its resources and management. This transition will affect not only the technology-related operations but will lead to changes in the way the shipping business operates. New kinds of capabilities will be required, and some actors may find their roles changed. Global companies' logistics chains are likely to become more integrated and adaptable using the whole fleet in an optimum way. Ongoing digitalization and autonomous technologies will create new services already along the way towards autonomous shipping. Some of these services will support existing market players and some will allow new players to enter the market. For example, in the automotive sector the self-driving car has been seen as an opportunity not only by traditional car manufacturers, but also by entrants from other technology sectors. The search is on for the best of the best technologies and the best is yet to come! In the next 10 to 15 years there will be a paradigm (positive) shift in sea trade and also the emergence of new trades, job opportunities and industries.

***

Chapter 2

Terms and Definitions

2.1 ISO Terms and Definitions Related to Autonomous Ships

These terms and definitions are compiled with reference to *Ships and Marine Technology - Vocabulary related to autonomous ship systems with reference to ISO/TS 23860:2022(en)*

Quote

3 Terms and definitions

ISO and IEC maintain terminology databases for use in standardization at the following addresses:

- — ISO Online browsing platform: available at https://www.iso.org/obp
- — IEC Electropedia: available at https://www.electropedia.org/

3.1 General terms

3.1.1

automatic

process or equipment that, under specified conditions, can function without human control

Note 1 to entry: See Annex B.1 for an explanation of the difference between **automation** (3.1.2) and **autonomy** (3.1.3).

[SOURCE:IEC 60050-351[4], modified – "can function" instead of "functions", added Note 1 to entry]

3.1.2

automation

implementation of processes by automatic means

[SOURCE:ISO/TR 11065[31]]

3.1.3

autonomy

processes or equipment in a ship system which, under certain conditions, are designed and verified to be controlled by automation, without human assistance

Note 1 to entry: Autonomy is implemented by automation but emerges when automation is designed and verified to allow operation without human assistance.

Note 2 to entry: This definition qualifies autonomy by giving it a temporal (the period when conditions are satisfied) and a process (one or more processes or equipment) dimension. The term "autonomy" on its own should be avoided unless sufficiently qualified with respect to what processes, period, or conditions it refers to.

Note 3 to entry: See Annex B.1 for an explanation of the difference between **automation** (3.1.2) and **autonomy** (3.1.3).

3.1.4

autonomous

possessing the property of autonomy

Note 1 to entry: Except when used in a general sense, e.g. a**utonomous ship system** (3.1.5), the term "autonomous" on its own should be avoided [refer also to Note 2 of **autonomy** (3.1.3)].

3.1.5

autonomous ship system

elements that interact to ensure effective functioning of the autonomous and non-autonomous processes and equipment that are necessary to perform the ship's operation or voyage

Note 1 to entry: The autonomous ship can depend on systems not located on the ship, e.g. communication systems, shore and port infrastructure, remote control centres etc.

Note 2 to entry: The autonomous ship system refers to a full system, including the ship. If the reference is made to the ship itself, the term "autonomous ship" or just "ship" can be used.

3.1.6

control

purposeful action on or in a process to meet specified objectives

[SOURCE:IEC 60050-351[4]]

Note 1 to entry: The term control does not preclude that the action is only to monitor the process, e.g. to raise an alarm or to request intervention. Control can be exercised by a human or by automation.

3.1.7

process

set of interrelated or interacting activities that transforms inputs into outputs

[SOURCE:ISO 9000[1]]

Note 1 to entry: Processes onboard a ship can correspond to function as defined in the International Convention on Standards of Training, Certification and Watchkeeping (STCW)[8]. Function means a group of tasks, duties and responsibilities, as specified in STCW, necessary for ship operation, safety of life at sea or protection of the marine environment.

3.1.8

remote control centre

site remote from the ship that can control some or all of the autonomous ship system processes

Note 1 to entry: A remote control centre may consist of more than one control room or stations that may be located at different physical locations. See ISO 11064-3[2] for a more extensive set of terminology for control rooms and centres.

Note 2 to entry: The terms shore control centre and remote operations centre are sometimes used to refer to remote control centres.

Note 3 to entry: When the abbreviated form of the term Remote Control Centre is used, i.e. RCC, one should be careful to avoid confusion with a Rescue Coordination Centre.

3.1.9

uncrewed

ship with no crew onboard

Note 1 to entry: Crew does not include passengers, special personnel etc.

3.1.10

unmanned

ship with no humans onboard

3.2 Terms related to autonomous ship system components

3.2.1

automatic facilities services

collection of automatic offshore services and automatic port services

3.2.2

automatic offshore services

fully or partly automatic services provided from an offshore facility or in the autonomous ship's operational area outside the port, that are defined as part of the autonomous ship system, but that are not located on the ship

Note 1 to entry: Automatic offshore services do not include local sensor systems or planned response services.

3.2.3

automatic port services

fully or partly automatic services provided in a port area, that are defined as part of the autonomous ship system, but that are not located on the ship

Note 1 to entry: Automatic port services do not include local sensor systems or planned response services.

3.2.4

autonomous onboard controller

automation onboard the ship that is used to control one or more of a ship system's processes or equipment, under certain conditions, without human assistance

3.2.5

autonomous remote controller

automation in the remote-control centre that is used to control one or more of a ship system's processes or equipment, under certain conditions, without human assistance

3.2.6

connectivity

network facilities to maintain communication between the ship and other parts of the autonomous ship system

3.2.7

local sensor systems

environment sensors and data processing systems located in the ship's local operating area, but off the ship, that provide additional data and/or information to the autonomous ship system's environment assessment functions

Note 1 to entry: This can be used, for example, to remove radar shadows, improve positioning accuracy and otherwise assist in complex operations, such as in high density traffic or during berthing.

3.2.8

planned response services

services provided by organizations with facilities not located onboard the ship, to assist in situations where the onboard systems are unable to handle the situation alone

Note 1 to entry: This may include, for example, towage in case of critical sub-system failure on board or evacuation services for passengers on an uncrewed ship.

3.3 Terms related to operations

3.3.1

tolerable event

technical or operational event for which there is a designed response that keeps the system within its operational envelope

Note 1 to entry: A tolerable event includes events that are part of routine operations as well as events that are not considered part of normal operation but occur in practice as a result of different operational contexts (e.g. heavy weather, damage, failures, reduced communications capabilities, operator errors, etc.).

3.3.2

operator control mode

working mode, sometimes supported by technology or procedures, that represents the expected class of actions performed by the crew or remote-control centre operators

Note 1 to entry: Modes can be changed during a voyage or operation and/or for specific functions.

Note 2 to entry: 3.4 defines four operator control modes.

3.3.3

fallback state

designed state that can be entered through a fallback function when it is not possible for the autonomous ship system to stay within the operational envelope

Note 1 to entry: Being in a fallback state should not result in an intolerable risk (frequency and severity of any consequence).

3.3.4

fallback function

means to reach a **fallback state** (3.3.3)

3.3.5

fallback space

set of all *fallback***states** (3.3.3)

3.3.6

operational envelope

conditions and related operator control modes under which an autonomous ship system is designed to operate, including all tolerable events

Note 1 to entry: The operational envelope should cover at least all relevant voyage or operation phases as well as all relevant autonomous ship system processes.

The conditions should include geographic or fairway conditions, environmental conditions, own ship conditions, traffic conditions, division of responsibility between human and *automatic control*, as well as any other factors that have a significant impact on the operation of the autonomous ship system.

Note 2 to entry: The operational envelope (OE) is inspired by the operational design domain (ODD) as defined in SAE J3016[5]. However, as the OE also includes operations under human control, and as the relationship between OE and fallbacks are somewhat different than for the ODD, it has been decided to not use the name ODD and rather call this operational envelope. See B.3 for further details.

3.3.7

system control tasks

process control tasks, implemented by automation and/or humans, that are required to sustainably operate the autonomous ship system within its operational envelope

Note 1 to entry: A process control task is the control task or function related to a specific process. The task or function can be automatic or performed by a human.

3.4 Terms related to operator control modes

3.4.1

monitoring

operations which monitor a situation but do not take any action to influence necessary processes.

Note 1 to entry: In monitoring mode, operators may adjust non-necessary processes or equipment to facilitate gathering of information. Monitoring can, for example, be to adjust a system for exclusively human use, such as external lights or cameras, or to inspect equipment or trends in performance parameters.

3.4.2

strategic control

operations to issue fleet-wide instructions that implement and, if appropriate, define specific functions to be used by the automatic decision-making units

Note 1 to entry: Strategic control corresponds to a Master's standing orders on a conventional ship.

3.4.3

tactical control

operations to influence the conclusion made by the automatic decision-making units of the autonomous ship for a particular purpose

Note 1 to entry: Tactical control includes, for example, changing the required minimum closest point of approach to other ships or the port of destination and letting the autonomous ship system afterwards construct the avoidance manoeuvre or route itself. It can also be adjustment of a technical alert level, based on prevailing conditions, for example, the time delay in actuation of the bilge alarm.

3.4.4

direct control

operations to control a specific function or parameter

Note 1 to entry: Direct control means, for example, that the operator changes a waypoint that would otherwise be decided by the autonomous ship systems directly, or that the operator selects and overrides the machinery standby configuration, such as changing of generator or pump standby status.

Unquote

***

Chapter 3

2025 and Beyond

3.1 Autonomous Ships and the Smart Marine Eco System

By now, we have read about the legislations, terms, and definitions. Simply put, any sea-going vessel that can navigate without human intervention and with the help of artificial intelligence programs is called an autonomous ship. This is a great step forward for the container and cargo shipping industry.

From 2025 onwards, once many committees have laid down their legislations and the ship-building industry and operators are more aligned to these in terms of acceptance and implementation from cradle to grave, the world will see many more autonomous ships enter and leave harbours.

Autonomous ships are constantly in the news because of their prospects to make sea freight shipping more profitable and even more agile. Moreover, they will also have a massive positive impact on the functioning of the ports.

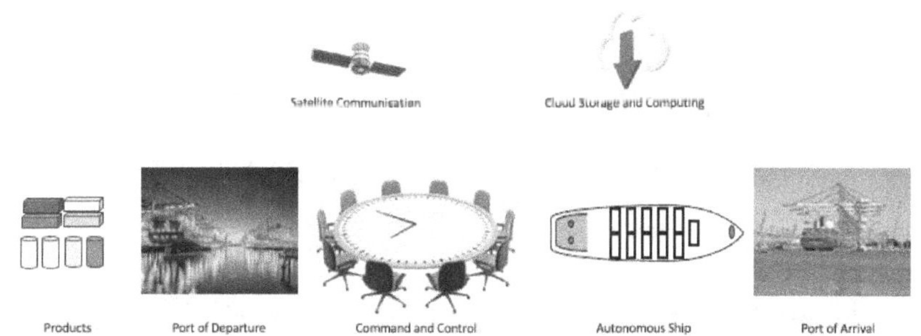

Figure 3.1 – Main Elements of the Smart Marine Eco System

Of course, there is much work to be done to make sure that automated ships are used safely. Just as automated trucks and cars are not roaming the streets on their own, crew-less ships won't take over the oceans the moment an automated ship gets built.

There are laws to consider, technology to be developed, logistics to be worked out... But these are coming in a very big way and with the support of the IMO and its members.

3.2 Infrastructure for Autonomous Ships

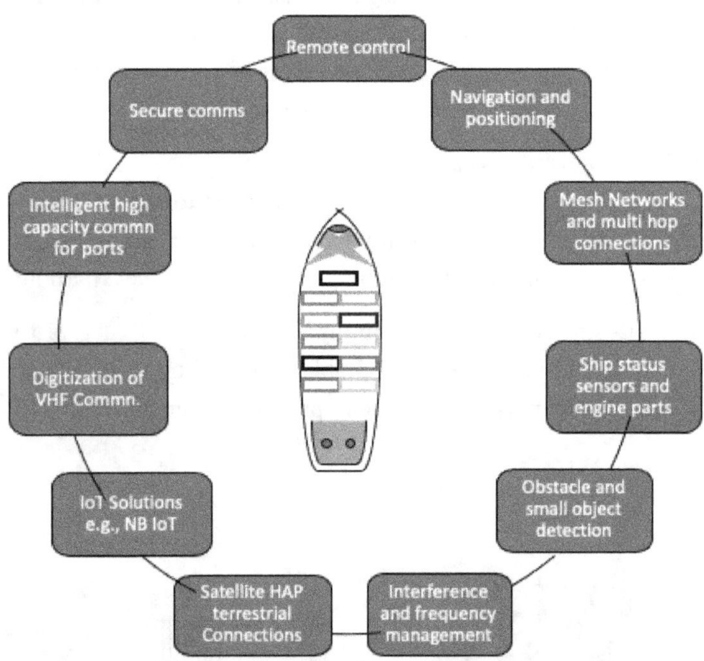

Figure 3.2 - Additional Infrastructure for Autonomous Ships

3.2.1 Remote Control Capabilities

UMS Ships with unmanned engine rooms, machinery spaces and bridges with auto pilots have been around for a long time, thus paving the way for remote control capabilities.

This debate, however, continues from one aspect to another, the main factor being the unpredictable sea and the weather conditions that make it very difficult at times.

Despite the numerous weather stations working round the clock, geographical surveys being done, meteorological experts' predictions being shared with the vessels, safe voyage planning being done, there are new surprises always. However, in extreme situations, even experienced seafarers cannot handle their vessels, but these are getting fewer. Statistics show that from the 52,000+ manned commercial vessels at sea, a very small percentage are still affected by human errors and bad sea conditions. Arguably, that is still huge sums of money lost by someone somewhere!

Today mankind has managed to remotely and / or automatically control toys, robots in restaurants, factories, shipyards, and warehouses, then there are driverless vehicles in heavy road traffic that are still evolving, drones with multiple capabilities, light aircrafts, missiles, torpedoes, submarines, spaceships, and the list goes on… so why not ships?

With the numerous communication protocols and mature control capabilities, the transition to the shipping environment is not going to be so difficult for those who want to try. That is why the longstanding companies and experienced / knowledgeable people have managed to move from the proof-of-concept stage to real ships doing real but limited trade now.

These days, the navigation of such ships is mostly in the coastal area and must be supervised by an Ashore Control Center (ACC) that manages a massive amount of data where it is received by decision-making systems and personnel that return navigation strategies to each ship in the area.

However, there can be conditions wherein no ACC is available to supervise the navigation of ships whether autonomous or manned and operating in the same sea area, thus resulting in a more challenging scenario.

To fit such a set of different situations, we can design a system that is represented in Figure 3.3 and includes the following entities: ships, sensors, AI algorithms and ACC. The sensors deployed in the navigation area will provide useful information to the ships, AI algorithms, and the ACC. Based on this information, the ship controller will plan or maintain the route to be followed.

The AI algorithms will enrich the data from sensors to support the ship's decisions and the monitoring at the ACC. Finally, the ACC merges data coming from sensors, from the vessels and the AI, to supervise and coordinate the traffic in the area of its competence. Moreover, as a failure backup strategy, ACC operators are equipped with an augmented-reality device, and they can monitor the situation and plan any manual interventions.

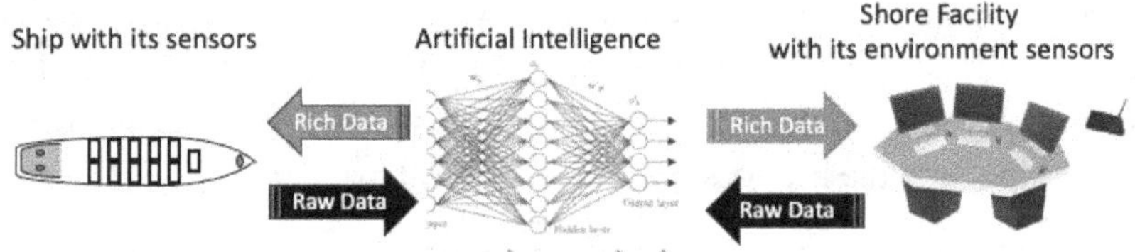

Figure 3.3 – The Influence of AI on Data Exchange

3.2.2 Layout of the Marine Traffic Management

Automatic route planning or advanced intelligent routing (AIR) is based on metocean data, traffic separation schemes and regional regulations on acceptable fuel types, using artificial intelligence technologies. Metocean data used in riser analysis are water depth, waves, currents, tide, surge variations and marine growth. For the extreme waves and currents, the 1, 10, 100-yr and higher return periods may be considered. The 95% non-exceedance values may be used as temporary installation design condition.

3.2.2.1 Benefits of AIR

- Connection to the eco system
- Fastest and safest route, including real-time updates
- Weather optimization
- Up to 5-7% fuel savings (Opex savings)
- Reduced bridge crew workload
- Safety check and voyage plan documentation
- Avoids congestion
- Enables just-in-time arrival at the port

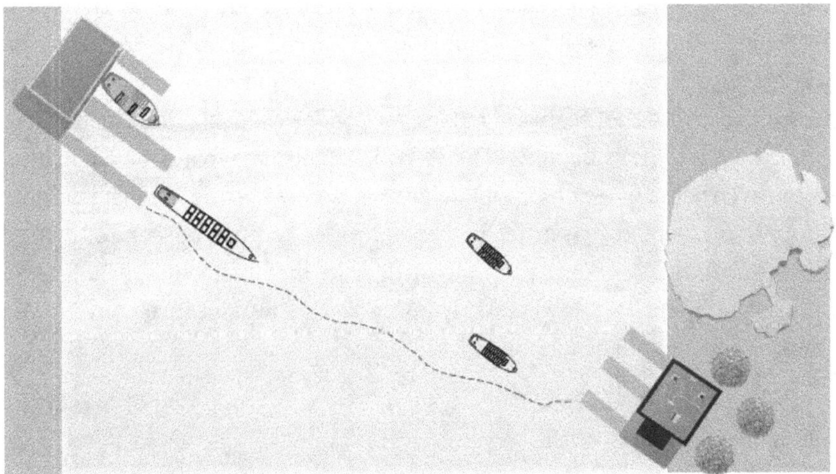

Figure 3.4 - Advanced Intelligent Routing for Autonomous Ships

For autonomous and remotely operated vessels to become a reality, several general challenges must be overcome, such as public acceptance, the development of rules and regulations, and acceptable / insurable risk levels.

The massive technology changes happening in the transportation sector will not only influence how cars, trucks and ships will be operated and controlled, but also how they are powered by cleaner energies.

The sensors installed on either ship or in the surrounding environment will be implemented following the Internet of Things paradigm that are to be easily accessible from all the involved entities.

Artificial Intelligence (AI) algorithms are needed to create an Intelligent System (IS) and improve the autonomous decision process. They can be deployed and executed either or both on the ships and at the ACC. This system improves situational awareness through the identification of obstacles and their possible classification. The considerable amount of data coming from multiple and diverse sources, acquired by heterogeneous sensors, enables the analysis and extraction of valuable information for monitoring specific situations. The IS will use this data to aid the navigation from two perspectives: on one side, it extracts new knowledge that is usable through augmented reality by the operators of the ashore control station dealing with the monitoring; on the other side, the obtained knowledge can be used onboard to allow the ship to carry out evasive manoeuvres and strategies in complete autonomy.

The control and supervisory systems layout is composed of two layers interacting with each other.

The remote one aims to coordinate the traffic, and the local one is needed to handle the single ship. For this purpose, a Guidance-Navigation-Control (GNC) system for autonomous navigation needs to be ready to receive external information. In particular, GNC using the results from the AI algorithms, can detect an obstacle (either fixed or moving), elaborate an optimum evasive route, and, thanks to its control system, can actuate the new route safely and accurately.

However, in the case of a failure on any single component of the VTS (vessel traffic service), the collision avoidance is still active; thanks to the local Guidance-Navigation-Control system. This solution will be clearly sub-optimal, since the coordination part with the other entities of the scenario will be missing.

Eventually, to support the operations in such a heterogeneous set of scenarios, an Orchestration and Communication Platform (OCP) will be developed to efficiently handle the interactions among the ISs and the GNCs residing on the same ship, on different ships, or also within the ashore control centre.

The OCP will provide flexibility to the overall system, allowing each ship for dealing efficiently with each scenario that can occur. For example, the vessel will discover whether other autonomous ships are navigating in the same area or if an ACC is available to monitor and support the traffic.

To achieve the proposed goals, the VTS needs to operate on three main aspects: autonomous maritime navigation, the analysis of a massive amount of data through AI, and the orchestration and management of their interactions. From the marine-engineering perspective, the main changes is a new layer that communicates with the AI algorithms, receives the raw data from sensors, and detects a potential collision.

In case a collision risk is detected, an optimised routing algorithm provides an evasive route. The optimisation problem is highly constrained and needs to consider the real manoeuvrability or ships' capability, weather conditions, propulsion plant and manoeuvring-device limits. Once a new route is assessed by employing way-points (two spatial coordinates plus time), coordinated and shared with the VTS, this information will be sent to the track-keeping module, that will perform the proper set-points to reach the way-point accurately and safely, as shown in Figure 3.4.

From the data analysis perspective, the VTS uses AI techniques to integrate and analyse various heterogeneous data, including raw measurements and images.

The AI algorithms are used to extract the information about obstacles or ships, mine the correlations between them, and build models that would enable predicting the route evolution. This rich data that is produced, supports both the GNC in executing its tasks and the a operators in their monitoring activity. The process will be fully automate; however, the information will be displayed at the ACC's for human-operators iwhioAugmented Reality techniques in case of any necessity.

This brings us to the next "in thing", which is the IoT solutions and of course more modern standards like Narrow Band IoT.

3.3 IIoT Solutions

Industrial IoT will be used to allow the various support agencies in the industry to connect in different geographies and time-zones to:

- Monitor plant performance from remote locations, and view all critical parameters through visual dashboards, in real-time.
- Enable Condition-based monitoring (CBM), and reduce expensive downtime, give warning of safety issues, and continuously monitor the health of machines
- Use remote cloud-based monitoring of installations to enable a high level of integration with customers.

Manage the over-whelming data overload. Unlock greater value through data and Connectivity.

Integrate all data to a common platform:

- Connect data from all machines and auxiliary equipment to an ERP system; access a management console for reports and analytics; download customized advanced reports on every ship.
- Tag, process, and store all data assets as well as of the millions of data points coming in every day from the machines and other digitalized systems of the fleet. Also sort and back-up all this data securely on the cloud.
- Use analytics to make sense of the data to predict customer needs in advance, trigger timely interventions, augment human capabilities, and control process efficiencies.

3.3.1 Latest NB-IoT Standard

Narrowband Internet of things (NB-IoT) is a low-power wide-area network (LPWAN) radio technology standard developed by 3GPP for cellular network devices and services. The specification was frozen in 3GPP Release 13 (LTE Advanced Pro – (Long Term Evolution)), in June 2016. Other 3GPP IoT technologies include eMTC (enhanced Machine-Type Communication) and EC-GSM-IoT. The 3rd Generation Partnership Project (3GPP) is an umbrella term for several standards organizations which develop protocols for mobile telecommunications. Its best-known work is the development and maintenance of: GSM and related 2G and 2.5G standards, including GPRS and EDGE.

LTE Advanced Pro (3GPP Release 13+) is expanding LTE to a wide range of new industries and enabling new use cases beyond smartphones, such as automotive and IoT. The goal in Release 13 is to expand LTE CA up to 32 CCs and hence provide a major leap in the achievable data rates for LTE as well as in the flexibility to aggregate large numbers of carriers in different bands.

NB-IoT focuses specifically on indoor coverage, low cost, long battery life, and high connection density. NB-IoT uses a subset of the LTE standard but limits the bandwidth to a single narrow-band of 200kHz. It uses OFDM modulation for downlink communication and SC-FDMA for uplink communications. IoT applications which require more frequent communications will be better served by LTE-M, which has no duty cycle limitations operating on the licensed spectrum. In March 2019, the Global Mobile Suppliers Association (GSA) announced that over 100 operators had either NB-IoT or LTE-M networks. This number had risen to 142 deployed / launched networks by September 2019.

3.3.1.1 Deployments

As of March 2019, GSA identified:

149 operators in 69 countries investing in one or both NB-IoT and LTE-M network technologies

- 104 of those operators in 53 countries had deployed / launched at least one of the NB-IoT or LTE-M technologies of those, 20 operators in 19 countries had deployed/launched both NB-IoT and LTE-M
- 22 countries are now home to deployed / launched NB-IoT and LTE-M networks
- 29 countries are home to deployed / launched NB-IoT networks only
- Two countries are home to deployed / launched LTE-M networks only
- operators in 69 countries investing in NB-IoT networks; 90 of those operators in 51 countries had deployed / launched their networks
- 60 operators in 35 countries investing in LTE-M networks; 34 of those operators in 24 countries had deployed / launched their network.

Note: *We are fast moving to 5G standards and other protocols that evolve on a case-by-case basis. Very soon the world will experience the power of 6G too!*

3.4 Navigation and Positioning

Auto pilot systems with voyage planning systems coupled to it, will help greatly in unmanned control of the steering system. Then there is ECDIS and Radars for the surface while Echo Sounders and Under Keel Clearance acoustic sensors that can help with safe navigation. Then of course the almost indispensable GPS and DGPS systems top it all!

While manoeuvring in harbours and busy shipping lanes, we need detection systems for close quarter navigation albeit at lower speeds, which brings us to exploring the use of anti-collision systems and sensors or object and small object detection systems.

3.5 Obstacle and Small Object Detection

The current situation is continuously updated, and real-time monitoring will be possible. Thus, identifying obstacles and ships will allow the motion-planning system to carry out appropriate manoeuvres and predict evasive routes.

Marine object detection and classification are two essential tasks for many applications such as vessel identification and positioning, collision avoidance system, safe autonomous navigation, search and rescue mission, etc. Marine objects can span from stationary floating objects such as buoys to small boats and kayaks and other large vessels such as ferries, passenger ships and cargo ships.

Surveillance adopting shared information from the Electronic Chart Display and Information System (ECDIS) and the Global Navigation Satellite System (GNSS) can provide the locations of marine vessels.

However, this depends on the reliability of data, which may degrade due to spoofing, jamming or even de-activating automatic identification systems (AIS). Radar-based methods can be effective to detect the presence of large vessels. Small boats and floating objects on the water's surface, are difficult to be identified.

Visual detection of marine objects using electro-optical sensors provides a solution for detecting and classifying marine objects. Classification and detection of objects using captured images have been widely used in several application domains.

However, the characteristics of the scenes captured in the marine environment arise additional challenges to the task of detecting objects in images or videos compared to other environments.

Factors such as dynamic nature of the background, unavailability of static cues, presence of small objects at distant backgrounds and illumination effects, impact the performance of commonly used image processing and computer vision approaches.

Tides and waves lead to a continuously dynamic background in both spatial and temporal dimensions. Also, floating objects are subjected to a lot of motion with unpredictable patterns.

The illumination of marine scenes varies due to weather conditions (haze, fog, rain, bright sunlight, twilight, etc.). Speckles and glints are mainly induced by the variation of the solar incident angle on water. Furthermore, the disparity of the colour range depends on illumination conditions. The colour range varies between dark yellow and red, blue and gray during night, sunset, daylight, and hazy conditions. These factors affect the visibility of objects in marine environments and hence detection performance is vital. An effective technique for certain cases with specific illumination type, weather condition and water dynamicity may not suit other conditions.

Artificial intelligence (AI) techniques based on deep learning provide robust solutions to detect and locate objects. The achieved performance proves the relevance of convolution neural networks (CNNs) in circumventing existing computer vision challenges.

Deep learning methods, known as deep neural networks, make use of multiple hidden layers between the input and output layers to learn a hierarchy of features that are invariant to geometric transformations from raw input images.

Previously, computer vision techniques based on feature extraction has been widely adopted to detect objects. Recently, AI methods with Convolutional Neural Networks play a dominant role in classifying and locating multiple objects in images and videos leading to accurate detection. One-stage detection methods have been introduced to provide real-time performance with acceptable precision and accuracy. These methods exclude the stage of pre-selecting the regions of classification and abstract post-processing techniques (refining bounding boxes, eliminating duplicates, and adjusting detection scores) used in two-stage methods such as the well-known region-convolutional neural network (R-CNN) and its enhanced versions to reduce the complexity and ensure real-time detection speed.

You Only Look Once (YOLO) has been recently proposed as an efficient one-stage CNN-based model that is able to detect multi objects in real-time. Published peer reviewed comparisons illustrate that YOLO outperforms two-stage detection methods and other available one-stage methods such as single shot detector (SSD).

Since introduced, many versions of YOLO have been introduced such as YOLOv2, YOLOv3, YOLOv4 and YOLOv5. In YOLOv2, the fully connected layers at the end have been eliminated and Darknet-19 architecture has been adopted.

YOLOv3 uses Darknet-53 architecture and inherits the concept of residual networks. The detections are made at 3 different scales which enables the detection of small objects. YOLOv4 and YOLOv4-tiny proposed initially in 2020 optimize and improve every part of YOLOv3.

The main optimization is to use CSPDarknet-53 as its backbone network for extracting features. The difference between YOLOv4-tiny and YOLOv4 is that the tiny version only has two YOLO heads at the end (2 scale factor instead of 3).

According to researchers, the experiments targeting Microsoft Common object in context (COCO) dataset show that YOLOv4 is faster and more accurate than real-time neural networks EfficientDet and RetinaNet provided by Google and Facebook respectively.

Comparisons have been made between YOLOv3, YOLOv4 and YOLOv5, in which some authors claim that YOLOv4 is more accurate while others claim that YOLOv5 is more accurate.

The reason for different reported results can be attributed to many factors, such as the different datasets used, the modified hyperparameters, etc.

3.5.1 Maritime Detection Datasets

Object detection based on deep learning imposes the challenge of having sufficient dataset with object annotations for training and validation processes. Training using large datasets with diverse images results in robust networks and prevents the occurrence of overfitting or underfitting.

In a maritime context, only few datasets for maritime object detection are available publicly for research purposes. This subsection presents briefly these available published datasets.

VAIS (vessel arrival information sheet) dataset provides visible and infrared maritime images for ship classification. It includes more than 1,000 paired RGB and infrared images among six ship categories (merchant, sailing, passenger, medium, tug, and small). The large-scale MARitime VEsseLs (MARVEL) dataset has been introduced for classification of maritime vessels. Although the dataset includes 2M images, the provided ground truth (GT) annotations contain the URL to download the image and the class label without bounding boxes. Also, the available scripts to retrieve the images from the Ships Spotting website is no longer functioning. Both VAIS and MARVEL datasets are not applicable for deep learning detection.

The merging of all datasets leads to 10K images split into 15 classes namely: ferry, buoy / seamark, sailing-vessel, tug, speed boat, kayak, bulk carrier, roro cargo, small boat, swimming person, flying bird, container ship, fishing vessel, passenger ship and jetski.

3.6 Mesh Networks and Multi-hop Connections

Mesh networks are regularly distributed networks that generally allow transmission only to a node's nearest neighbours. The mesh networks can also be referred to as peer-to-peer networks since the network nodes are assumed to be identical.

Even though all nodes may be identical and have the same computing and transmission functionalities, certain mesh nodes can be designated as mesh group leaders which then take on additional leadership functions to form a mesh network.

If a group leader is suddenly disabled, another node will then inherit, and take over these group leadership duties, recovering the disabled network in a real-time fashion.

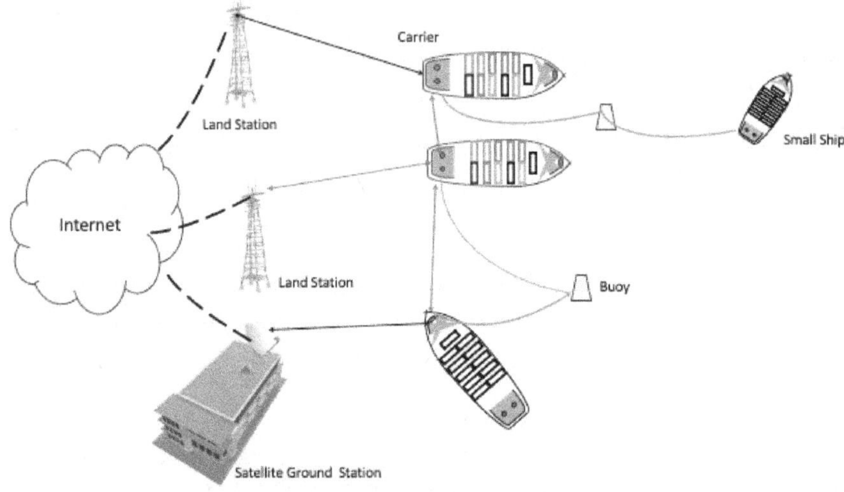

Figure 3.5 – A Mesh Network

Mesh networks are, therefore, good models for expanding existing terrestrial networks to form large-scale maritime networks which are distributed over a wide range with buoys. To maintain backward compatibility with the existing maritime communications deployment and to guarantee reliable maritime communications, legacy maritime communications systems are integrated as part of maritime wireless mesh networks (MWMNs). The goal is to build an integrated maritime communications network in which mesh and satellite as well as radio communications resources can be used in an optimum way to provide the best possible overall communications capability for maritime users.

The TRITON network has developed a ship-to-ship and ship-to-shore mesh network that provides an alternative high-speed communications network which can operate reasonably well in busy shipping lanes, narrow water channels and traffic lanes close to shorelines. In TRITON, the coverage extension is achieved by forming a wireless multi-hop network amongst neighboring ships, marine beacons and buoys using wireless communications technology (WiMAX). The multi-hop wireless network is connected to the terrestrial networks via land stations, which are placed at regular intervals along the shoreline. The TRITON network resembles a vehicular ad-hoc network (VANET) but with some unique characteristics given by the distinct ship mobility pattern, position awareness of neighboring ships via the automatic identification system (AIS), wave rocking movement and wave occlusion due to sea surface.

A nautical ad-hoc network (NANET) has shown a possibility of forming a mesh and / or ad-hoc network in the case of establishing maritime networks on (near) the shore or in the ocean. The proposed network considers specific factors for maritime communications, such as mobility and the route of the ship, ship density at sea, and ocean wave fluctuation.

A maritime communications network is basically a heterogenous network which may consist of cellular communications and satellite mobile communications such as the integrated wireless maritime communications network (IWMCN). Maritime-Manet is introduced as a network concept for communications between maritime platforms such as vessels, commercial ships, or buoys. The network is based on multiple directive antennas for transmission, which is the key difference from the conventional approach to the ad-hoc networks that uses omnidirectional antennas. The former approach provides a much longer transmission range in the maritime environment.

Another example of the maritime communications network is the MarCom network, which aims at developing an innovative digital communications system to overcome the lagging of mobile network applications in the maritime environment.

The main objectives of the MarCom project are to extend the network coverage and range at sea for the conventional and novel terrestrial wireless systems and technologies, integrate digital satellite communications (SATCOM) to provide coverage beyond the terrestrial capability and to obtain a smooth transition between the systems.

There are several maritime safety and security systems mandated by the international maritime organization (IMO). These systems include AIS and the global maritime distress and safety system (GMDSS). The GMDSS allows a ship to send a message if it is in danger through several means to ensure a due response. The GMDSS is a heterogeneous system which uses medium frequency (MF), high frequency (HF), VHF and maritime satellite (COSPAT-SARSAT). The mentioned systems have low bandwidth, which limits the exchange of data to the extent of transferring essential navigation data required to improve safety and security at sea. E-navigation has been proposed by the IMO to enhance safety, security, and protection of the maritime environment. The concept utilizes electronic means to improve the collection, integration, exchange, presentation, and analysis of maritime information.

The e-navigation system requires a high-speed and cost-effective maritime wireless communications link to be a successful radical departure from the conventional maritime communications systems.

Traditionally, maritime networks are useful in naval task group deployments, but they are equally applicable to other maritime activities such as commercial fishing, shipping, emergency operations, or coast guard duties. Typically, as shown in Figure 3.6, for such deployment, a relatively small number of maritime nodes (ships) are dispatched in small groups. A satellite ground base station installed ashore provides access to server-based application services and acts as a satellite switching center.

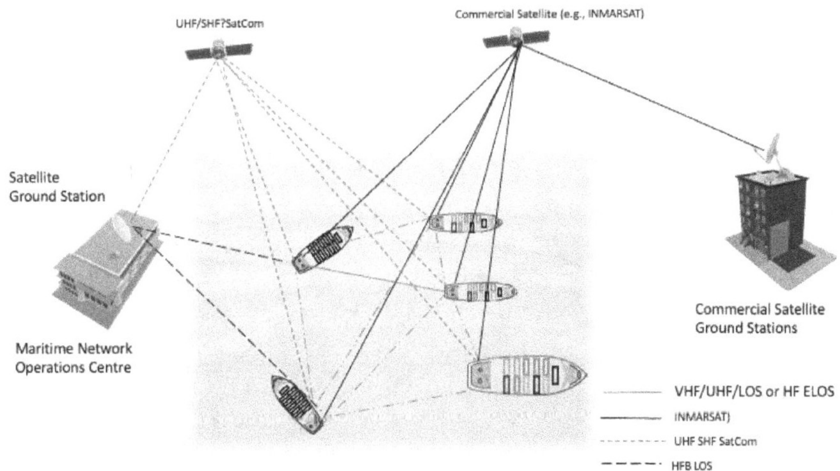

Figure 3.6 – Shore Support Centres Serve as Satellite Ground Base

Basic maritime mesh networks consist of a network operational center (NOC) acting as a land-based relay for all satellite communications, a limited number of mobile nodes (ships or potentially maritime land/air units), and the links connecting them.

The communication links available to transfer information within the network include ship-to- shore satellite networks (e.g., super-high frequency (SHF) and (SATCOM)), commercial satellite (e.g., INMARSAT B), high-frequency (HF) beyond line-of-sight (BLOS), HF extended LOS (ELOS), and UHF/VHF line-of-sight (LOS). Most nodes in maritime networks communicate using a combination of two communications modes.

First, network nodes may communicate back to their home network via the NOC using satellite communications which can also be relayed at the NOC to provide indirect ship-to-ship communications. Satellite communications provide high bandwidth but high-delay and high-cost communications. Second, ships communicate directly with other ships via limited range radio. The UHF / VHF relay technology has been improved to the point that LOS radio systems may form mobile ad-hoc networks (MANETs).

In PACTOR-III, the MF / HF bands modem can cover up to 40, 000 km with the data rate of 9.6 kbps, whereas the typical coverage for VHF band modem is 4, 000 km with the data rate of 14.4 kbps.

If one ship has neighboring ships within 30 km, a mesh or an ad-hoc network can be formed using multi-hop communications. But, if there are no neighboring ships within 30 km, it is impossible to form mesh or ad-hoc network. Since the allocation of the VHF band for maritime communications in the 2007 world radiocommunication conference (WRC), new maritime communication systems have been developed in addition to AIS. AIS is a telematic system in the maritime environment which performs automatic data exchange among ships mainly used as an additive source of information for collision avoidance by ships, ship identification by shore-based vessel traffic services (VTS) and ship location.

AIS automatically and periodically broadcasts static and dynamic data of ships, such as position, velocity, length of the ship, destination port, and expected time of arrival as well as short safety messages. PACTOR-III is an example of maritime communications systems which use MF/HF band with typical coverage range 4,000-40, 000 km.

AIS also uses a VHF band, which adopts self-organized time division multiple access (SOTDMA) to prevent collision and provides safety voyage by transporting the information about the ships.

The maritime communications systems which use MF/HF and VHF bands enjoy the advantage of long transmission distance without the support of high data rate service.

The maritime wireless mesh network that enables the extension of the terrestrial network to the sea will complement or replace the existing high-cost satellite communications. In highly dense harbours and navigation channels, ships mobility is restricted by shipping lane directions and traffic laws.

Ships can skew at pre-assigned areas within a fixed minimum and maximum speed shipping lane. The shipping lanes will strict the network topology. Ships have rich power supply for onboard communications and localization equipment.

The wireless mesh network (WMN), which is a communications network made up of radio nodes structured in a mesh topology, has emerged as a key technology for next-generation wireless networking.

Industrial standards, such as IEEE 802.11 and IEEE 802.16, are all actively working on new specifications for WMNs. A WMN also provides basic networking infrastructure for communications in maritime mesh network. Some of the benefits of using WMNs in maritime wireless mesh networks are highlighted as follows:

Increased communications reliability and automatic network connectivity: Since redundant paths usually exist in WMNs, network robustness against potential problems, e.g., node failures and path failures can be improved.

Furthermore, a WMN is self-organized and self-configured. This feature is crucial for maritime communications networks automation, since it enables MWMNs to cope with new connectivity requirements driven by maritime nodes demands.

Large coverage and high data rate: WiMAX mesh network can enable both long distance and high data rate communications. The IEEE 802.16 is a wireless broad-band standard designed for long range wireless metropolitan area network (WMAN). In MWMNs, a large amount of critical information and social activities onboard ships is exchanged. Therefore, a communications network with large coverage and high data rate is necessary.

Technically, maritime networks and wireless mesh networks (WMN) are two different concepts. In the physical layer, IEEE 802.16 uses OFDM and at the media access control (MAC) layer, the channel access is performed by time-division-multiple-access (TDMA). A mesh network supported by the standard (e.g. IEEE 802.16d) allows network node to communicate directly with each other without the coordination of the base station even if the network nodes are not within the coverage of the base station.

A wireless multi-hop network can be created since the network nodes will cooperate in data exchange. In terrestrial wireless systems, the base stations installation will help in deploying the network.

However, the same approach cannot be implemented at sea where the ships can be scattered. The frame structure of the mesh networking consists of a control sub-frame and data sub-frame. The control messages will be conveyed in the control sub-frame in a free-collision scheduling mechanism. The data sub-frame is divided into 256 slots. The transmission time for each packet must be defined before relaying out the packet. The definition of transmission time is based on a distributed or a centralized algorithm.

In the distributed scheduling algorithm, network nodes forward their resource allocation bitmap through control packet. Avoiding contention and interference in data exchange is achieved by three-way handshake manner which is based on the resource allocation information. In the three-way handshake resource allocation manner, the transmitter node sends a bandwidth request to the receiver node initially; the receiver node responds by allocating the resources according to the resource bitmap and sends back the endowment allocation.

Upon receiving the reply from the receiver node, the transmitter node rebroadcasts the allocated resources to its neighbors for collision and interference mitigation. The resource allocation bitmap will be updated for the nodes receiving the grant or grant confirmation.

In the centralized scheduling algorithm, the network node sends a bandwidth request to its respective base station. Then, the base station will send the allocated time slot resources to the corresponding nodes. The centralized scheduling algorithm allows resource allocation via multi-hop.

The network nodes relay bandwidth request and acquire information for other network nodes. Generally, delays will be associated to the bandwidth allocation if the requesting network node is further away from the base station.

The concentration of the routing tree will affect the selection of the scheduling algorithm. If the tree is not large, centralized scheduling algorithm is better. However, if the routing tree is deep, then distributed scheduling algorithm is better due to the associated delay of the centralized scheduling algorithms.

The following sub-sections introduce networks which use WMN technology to extend the terrestrial network to the sea environment and support reliable maritime communications:

a) Nautical Ad-hoc Network A typical coverage for a base station provides optimum transmission with a single hop. Therefore, the present cellular systems or wireless point-to-point systems will only benefit ships in certain circumstances such as busy ports and narrow navigation channels.

   Mesh technology addresses the coverage of ships beyond the cellular systems capability. Recently, mesh technology has been actively researched for the terrestrial mobile wireless systems.

   There are several standards that adopt mesh technology in IEEE. However, the empirical application of these standards in the maritime environment has not been widely deployed. As a result of a conducted market survey that relies on real ship mobility models, the transmission range of a well-connected mesh network is at least 18 km.

The IEEE 802.16 mesh standard is released for a wireless metropolitan access network (MAN) with a typical coverage that can vary to 50 km. From a coverage perspective, this standard is suitable for the maritime mesh network. The result of some conducted research experiments shows that, given an antenna height of 16 m and IEEE 802.16e, broadband transmission in a Maritime ship-to-ship environment can extend up to a range of 45 km.

If a ship is surrounded by another within 30 km, a mesh / adhoc network can be created using a VHF modem to build multi-hop network connections. However, if no ship falls within its coverage of 30 km, then it is not possible to form the mesh or ad-hoc network. As a result, MF/HF modem activates dual-mode operation, which can cover up to 40, 000 km with the data rate of 9.6 kbps.

Through three different nautical ad-hoc network (NANET) configuration scenarios, this network is configured on harbor, shore, and in the ocean.

A NANET covers a harbor using an existing terrestrial communications network which can be extended by installing base stations across the coast.

Ships under the coverage of a base station on a shore can directly communicate with this base station.

If, however, the ship is located outside the coverage of the base station, i.e., there is no direct link to the base station, then a mesh network can be formed with other ships / buoys to reach the base station.

As mentioned above that the mesh network can be implemented with various wireless and radio communications technologies, such as IEEE 802.11, WiMAX IEEE 802.16e, and long-term evolution cellular network (LTE).

When ships are far away from the shore in the ocean, they cannot reach the base stations on the coast, and henceforth ships through mesh networks can establish peer-to-peer communications to reach the base stations.

Note that if there are no ships within the ship's coverage distance of the VHF modem, then the existing MF/HF modem can be employed which can allow a transmission distance up to 40,000 km, so that a direct communication with the base station can be achieved. In the NANET architecture, the difference between mesh, and ad-hoc network is the existence of the base station under the former approach. However, the low coverage of the VHF modem will hinder the establishment of the mesh/ad-hoc network. Therefore, the dependency on MF/HF in this network for the ocean scenario limits the practical implementation of NANET.

b) TRITON High Speed Maritime Mesh Network TRITON network devises a novel maritime architecture for establishing a high bandwidth maritime network which can guarantee the QoS levels required for maritime nodes in busy and narrow shipping lanes along the coastal areas. The TRITON network is based on a market survey compiled from different potential users ranging from commercial vessels, petroleum enterprises to civilian sea transportation ships to collect the requirements needed for a feasible maritime broad-band wireless network.

c) The WiMAX wireless technology is used in the network core architecture to establish a multi-hop maritime mesh network among neighboring ships, marine lighthouses, and buoys.

The maritime mesh network is integrated with the terrestrial networks through base stations placed along the coast at regular intervals. A maritime node (ship) carries a configurable mesh radio device which has the capability of switching the operating frequency depending on the geographical locations or sea conditions.

When these nodes are getting near port waters, the operating frequencies are limited to the terrestrial base stations. The satellite is integrated with the conceived architecture to provide communications for a low distribution of ships, since the mesh network is ideal for sufficient ships. This, however, places a limitation when there is a low distribution of ships, hence, the relaying transmission medium will be switched to a satellite link.

A continued link quality measurement is performed, and a switching middleware automatically switches the link based on the provided measurement since acceptable QoS level is the desired aim of the network.

d) Integrated Wireless Maritime Communication Network: The proposed integrated wireless maritime communication network (IWMCN) is composed of two parts namely cellular communications part and satellite mobile communications. This enables network nodes to communicate among them using cellular communications or a satellite mobile network through a network gateway.

Based on this maritime wireless communications network, several maritime systems have been developed to reliably support maritime communications. An integrated maritime service system (IMSS) provides various value-added services such as navigation, distress warning, voice communications, positioning, weather forecasting, and recreation.

Users' mobility is managed through virtual home environment (VHE) in 3G-IP multimedia sub-system (IMS). VHE is a concept of personal service environment portability among network boundaries and between terminals. In VHE, within the capabilities of any network and any terminal, users are presented with the same personalized attributes, user interface customization and services wherever the user is located.

Concerning VHE services, user data profile is stored in the home subscriber server (HSS).

Aligning with the subscriber profiles, HSS performs authorization and authentication of the user, provides information about the location of the subscriber and IP information. The positions of mobile users onboard can be supplied to HSS through onboard satellite gateway and satellite network.

In the IWMCN architecture, ships forming an ad-hoc network considered as a transit network in the ship-to-shore communications network and transmission network in ship-to-ship communications network.

A satellite is connected to an ad-hoc ship network via shipborne satellite gateway (SGW) and connects to the cellular communications system via terrestrial gateway (TGW). The IEEE 802.11s wireless mesh network standard is used to implement ship- to-ship ad hoc network.

The IEEE 802.11 standard enables mesh clients to communicate directly with each another and access the network through multiple mesh access points (MAPs).

Different network domains can be connected through MAPs which establish mesh links with each other over the path determined by a routing protocol.

A hybrid wireless mesh protocol (HWMP) based on ad-hoc on-demand distance vector (AODV) and Tree-based routing is considered as the default protocol in IEEE 802.11s.

To form an ad-hoc network among ships, initially, each ship sets up a MAP, where a single-hop wireless link is created among neighboring ships. MAPs transmit at adjustable power according to the quality of the path among adjacent MAPs to enable radio signals to reach neighbor MAPs.

When an ad-hoc network is formed among ships, data exchange can be performed through standard IP protocol and ship-to-ship voice and video communications can be established. Ships can be equipped with a positioning system such as GPS or GALILEO receiver terminal integrated with electronic chart display and information system (ECDIS) which sends positioning information to other ships within ad-hoc network connecting ships.

The selection of the communications system is based on the service requirements for ship-to-shore or ship-to-ship communications, which depends mainly on the condition of each communications system within the network and the location of the ships.

Algorithm 1 summarizes the selection of communications system procedure. For ship-to-ship communications, if the mobile user is within VANET between ships, then VANET will be selected to establish a connection. For ship-to-shore communications, if the mobile user is within the coverage of the cellular system, then a radio link can be established using cellular system.

However, if the user is not within the coverage of the cellular system, the satellite network will be utilized to establish a connection. IWMCN depends on the coverage of the cellular system to reduce the usage of the satellite system.

Hence, in the ocean scenario, i.e. when the mobile user is far away from the shore and if the cellular system does not consider optimizing its coverage extension to the sea, the involvement of the satellite network will increase the cost associated to this network.

Another drawback of IWMCN is when a connection needs to be established for ship-to-ship communications and when the mobile user is not located within VANET, then how the IWMCN will handle the selection of the communications link

e) Maritime Manet

A distributed surveillance application can be deployed in Maritime Manet network which provides uninterrupted surveillance over a large maritime area of responsibility (AoR).

The distributed surveillance application called sensors in concert (SiC) has been developed due to the inefficient and expensive existing maritime surface surveillance using satellites, maritime petroleum aerial vehicles, or multiple navy vessels.

SiC nodes create SiC systems, each node senses its surroundings up to 18 km using radar, automatic identification system, optionally equipment operator (EO), and passive sonar to communicate with its neighboring nodes to exchange sensor data and integrates its own sensor data with the other received sensors data using MaritimeManet.

SiC nodes can be conveyed over buoys, relatively small navy vessels, unmanned surface vehicles (USV), commercial ships, or oil rigs. SiC nodes should be placed at sufficient height so that the optical horizon complements the sensing range to achieve suitable spatial deployment which results in continuous and full coverage of area-of-responsibility (AoR) even when islands exist.

To enable SiC, maritime nodes should be able to communicate in an ad-hoc network manner. The underlining protocol of SiC nodes operates in three parts:

The distribution middleware sub-system (transport layer), the ad-hoc IP (MANET, SSM, DiffServ) sub-system (network layer), and the transmission sub-system (data link and physical layers).

A publish-subscribe data-oriented distribution middleware provides interconnection between different application processes. In the network layer, an ad-hoc routing protocol is used jointly with other IP forwarding capabilities such as protocol independent multi-casting with source specific multicast (PIM-SSM) and differentiated services (DiffServ).

With a novel approach of neighbors' discovery, LOS communications between nodes relies on multi-beam antennas. For beyond line-of-sight (BLOS) communications, an alternative wireless technology based on HF and near vertical indices skywave (NVIS) antenna is used when LOS is not supporting a connected network. The ad-hoc routing protocol will be defined by one of the available routing protocols of MANET.

Obviously, nodes are located on surface platforms with moderate speed and non-rapid changes in the network typology. To optimize routing protocol, modifications must be applied to a proactive protocol such as open link state routing (OLSR)

In MaritimeManet, each node transmits data to the nodes when they need it. The coordination and forwarding methods for data transmission can be configured using existing IP capabilities.

In the distribution middleware, a node publishes its data types defined by a data model and irrespective of the designed system to other nodes which can show interest in one or more of them.

The source-specific multi-cast (SSM) is the bearer for data dissemination where a unique data delivery channel is created by the IP-address of the source and the group addresses. Also, data types are uniquely mapped to group addresses.

Deficiency arises as this method operates well only in systems with multiple nodes having the same capabilities such as SiC despite that, SSM uses multicast forwarding which is utilized for communications sessions between two nodes. SSM must be activated in the network to use the source address and the group addresses channels.

Therefore, internet group management protocol (IGMP) is essential to permit nodes to join and receive packets from a certain channel. The delivery tree for the group addresses will be formulated by SSM routing protocol.

To use the channel, multicast forwarding is needed to exchange data. By using SSM in state of the ordinary multicast where any node can send to a multicast group avoids the exploitation of complex multi-cast routing. In SSM, unicast routing protocols adequate.

In MaritimeManet, the loss and delay values for specific data types' of service quality that can be tolerated foreach data type are achieved during forwarding in the network. Based on the control bits in the packet header, DiffServ allows controlling over the buffering of packets.

Prior to the packet forwarding over the network, a node maps the indicated loss and delay values to the best matching forwarding service and sets the controlling bit in the header.

The control bits deal with the delay and discard priorities of the packet. During the transmission of the packet at each intermediate node, the control bits decide how packets are treated in the queue.

By doing this, simple and efficient service differentiation is achieved with applications while guaranteeing their QoS requirements.

3.7 Ship's Status Sensors, Early Warning Systems

9 different major sensors that can be found in one form or another on each vessel, and information from which is used not only by the captains of the vessel to make decisions on manoeuvring but also by the shipping company to monitor vessel performance. They are as follows:

1. Speed log
2. Echo sounder
3. RPM and torque meter
4. Shaft motor
5. Thrust meter
6. Rudder indicator
7. Stabilizer fins
8. Wind anemometer
9. GPS

Chapter 3

Condition-based monitoring systems are installed in the entire vessel – especially the machinery spaces, which are beyond the scope of this book. However, they are explained in the Instrumentation and Control Made Easy Series of Elstan's® Pocketbook Series. These will have the following advantages:

- Maximize revenues
- Reduce expensive down-time
- Synchronize maintenance with scheduled downtime
- Reduce total cost of maintenance
- Eliminate secondary damages due to catastrophic breakdowns
- Perform tasks only when warranted
- Maximize safety and thus alleviate accidents
- Use data analytics to anticipate issues with each system

Cyber Physical System-based components enable asset owners to make dynamic adjustments of maintenance activities while considering the risks and costs associated with it:

✓ Using data mining techniques from CPS data, predictive algorithms can predict which component is likely to fail and when.

✓ Support maintenance personnel by easily identifying components which are most likely to fail.

✓ Due to this real-time monitoring of components, a continuous improvement of operations is possible.

✓ Increased availability of assets and reduced unplanned downtime.

✓ Creates opportunities for new business models such as Maintenance as a Service MaaS.

3.8 Interference and Frequency Management

A critical component of any unmanned and autonomous ship is wireless communication system that supports efficient and safe operations.

Multiple wireless systems are needed for resilient operations to fulfill capacity, latency, and secure communication needs. A hybrid connectivity concept that integrates satellite and terrestrial system components is defined and its components described in the following article.

An essential part of the concept is a connectivity manager that ensures quality of service (QoS) for communications.

3.9 Satellite-HAP-Terrestrial Connections

The explosion of data traffic and the users' demand for reliable and high-capacity connectivity pose great challenges to traditional wireless communication systems.

The existing terrestrial communication system with unsolved issues such as the shortage of available bandwidth and the limited back haul capacity of terrestrial small cells can hardly meet such transmission demand. To make up for such deficiency, low-earth-orbit (LEO) satellite networks operating over high-frequency bands have attracted increasing attention since they can provide wide-bandwidth and high-capacity data. However, severe path loss and long communication delay remain to be the development bottleneck of satellite networks.

Fortunately, the emergence of the high-altitude platform (HAP) overcomes such deficiencies of satellite communications. HAPs are stations located on aerial vehicles at an altitude of 20 to 50 km, aiming at exploiting the potential benefits of intermediate altitudes between terrestrial networks and satellite networks.

The integration of HAPs and terrestrial networks can provide high-capacity data services, with a reduction in delay and complexity compared with satellite networks.

Therefore, HAPs can serve as a promising communication method to assist satellite-terrestrial networks. Specifically, HAPs support dual-band connectivity. First, it can communicate with terrestrial users over C-band directly.

Second, it can provide ground user terminals (UTs) with data backhaul services over Ka-band.

Each UT acts as an access point that can transmit the users' data to the core network via LEO-based backhaul or HAP-based backhaul over the Ka-band. Most existing works only focus on the two-layer HAP-terrestrial networks, and only a few consider the three-layer satellite-HAP-terrestrial networks.

3.10 Digitization of VHF Systems

Communication between ships and the shore has taken place traditionally using a VHF radio. VHF radio equipment is used for shipping both at sea and inland. Over the years, the use of the VHF radio, and the wish to communicate and be sure that your message is received and understood, has grown. Digitisation in other areas of communication has improved the way we communicate (GSM, LTE etc.). But, in the marine bands, the introduction of new digital communication channels for data has put pressure on the availability of VHF voice channels. With the introduction of VDES (VHF Data Exchange System) a problem arises that this would not be an easy task to contend with.

The ITU (International Telecommunication Union) has taken the decision that the frequencies for VDES are available from 1st of January 2017 in the World Radio Conference of 2015.

The Netherlands has foreseen the same problems as they encountered; they sent in a paper to MSC97 to raise awareness of this problem. Due to this, IMO (International Maritime Organization) agreed that from the 1st of January 2024, these frequencies should be freed by Contracting States and VDES could then use these frequencies.

In the World Radio Conference of 2019 ITU also decided on the use of frequencies for VDES satellite communication.

For situational awareness it is commonly known that eyesight, VHF radio and radar are the main tools to accomplish this. Since 2003 AIS was added to serve as additional information to the radar or ECS or ECDIS. The main purpose is collision avoidance.

3.11 Intelligent High-Capacity Communication in Port Areas

Before delving into the advancements that are transforming port communications, it is essential to understand why efficient communication is crucial for ports. Here are some key reasons:

- ***Optimized Operations:*** Efficient port communications minimize downtime, shorten vessel turnaround time, and optimize resource allocation, improving overall operational efficiency.
- ***Enhanced Safety:*** Effective communication systems ensure timely coordination and response to potential safety hazards, reducing accidents and enhancing port safety.

- ***Improved Customer Experience:*** Smooth communication channels enable faster cargo handling, reducing wait times and enhancing customer satisfaction.
- ***Cost Reduction:*** Streamlined port communications result in lower operational costs due to reduced delays, improved resource utilization, and better planning.

3.11.1 Transformative Port Communication Innovations

Let's explore some of the innovative technological solutions that are revolutionizing port communications:

1. Internet of Things (IoT)

The IoT is reshaping the way ports operate by connecting various devices and sensors through the internet, enabling real-time data exchange and automation. Key advantages include:

- Remote monitoring and control of port infrastructure, such as cranes and gate systems, minimizing human intervention.
- Efficient asset tracking and logistics management, reducing the chances of theft or lost cargo.
- Predictive maintenance of machinery, optimizing maintenance schedules and reducing downtime.

2. Blockchain Technology

Blockchain technology provides a secure and transparent platform for recording and sharing port-related information. Key benefits include:

- Enhanced supply chain transparency, allowing stakeholders to track the movement of goods in real-time and reducing the risk of fraud.

- Immutable and tamper-proof data records, ensuring the validity and integrity of information shared between different entities.
- Simplification of trade processes, reducing paperwork and administrative burden through digitization.

3. Artificial Intelligence (AI)

AI is playing a transformative role in port communications by automating various processes and enabling intelligent decision-making.

Advantages of AI

- Efficient resource allocation through predictive analytics, optimizing port operations based on historical and real-time data.
- Automated inspection and maintenance, ensuring equipment is functioning optimally and preventing potential failures.
- Improved vessel traffic management, reducing congestion and enhancing overall port efficiency.

By embracing these transformative innovations, ports can streamline their operations, increase efficiency, and better adapt to the ever-evolving demands of global trade.

3.11.2 Future-Proofing Ports: Advancements in Communication Technology for Streamlined Operations

3.11.2.1 The Power of 5G Networks

One of the most significant advancements in communication technology for ports is the advent of 5G networks.

With faster speeds, higher capacity, and ultra-low latency, 5G enables real-time data exchange, which is crucial for optimizing port operations.

Here are some key advantages of 5G in the port industry:

- ***Improved Efficiency:***

  5G enables real-time monitoring and control of critical port infrastructure, such as container cranes and gate operations, leading to increased efficiency and productivity.

- ***Enhanced Safety:***

  With 5G-powered IoT devices and sensors, port operators can monitor and respond to potential safety hazards in real-time, minimizing the risks of accidents.

- ***Enhanced Communication*** and ***Smart Traffic Management:***

  5G networks facilitate intelligent traffic management systems between autonomous vehicles and equipment, boosting operational efficiency., enabling ports to optimize the flow of goods, reduce congestion, and improve overall logistics.

- ***Rapid Data Transfer***

  Real-time monitoring and control of port operations, ensuring prompt decision-making.

- ***Optimized Asset Management:*** The ability to collect and analyse real-time data from various port assets enables predictive maintenance, reducing downtime and optimizing the lifespan of equipment.

- ***Seamless integration of emerging technologies like AI and machine learning***

  This leads to advanced data analytics for better port management.

3.11.3 Industrial Internet of Things (IIoT)

The Industrial Internet of Things (IIoT) plays a crucial role in future-proofing ports by connecting various devices, equipment, and infrastructure to the internet. By harnessing the power of IIoT, ports unlock a wealth of benefits such as:

- ***Real-Time Monitoring:*** IIoT sensors embedded within port infrastructure provide real-time insights into operational processes, allowing for proactive decision-making.
- ***Increased Efficiency:*** IIoT enables the automation of tasks, reducing manual labour and streamlining workflows, leading to improved operational efficiency.
- ***Condition Monitoring:*** Sensors can monitor the condition of port assets, such as cranes and containers, helping identify potential issues before they escalate, thus preventing costly damages.
- ***Optimized Energy Management:*** By analysing data from various devices, IIoT can optimize energy consumption in ports, leading to significant cost savings.

3.11.4 Artificial Intelligence (AI) and Machine Learning (ML)

The integration of Artificial Intelligence (AI) and Machine Learning (ML) technologies in port operations brings automation and predictive capabilities to a whole new level. Here's how AI and ML are transforming the port industry:

- ***Automated Decision-Making:*** AI algorithms can process vast amounts of data and make real-time decisions, assisting port operators in optimizing processes and resource allocation.

- ***Predictive Analytics:*** By analysing historical data, AI and ML models can predict maintenance needs, vessel arrival times, and supply chain disruptions thus enabling proactive planning.
- ***Optimized Resource Allocation:*** AI-based systems can determine the most efficient use of resources, such as labour, vehicles, and storage space, resulting in cost savings and increased productivity.
- ***Risk Management:*** AI-powered systems can identify potential risks, weather conditions, or security threats, allowing port authorities to take preventive measures and mitigate any negative impact.

3.11.5 Seamless Connectivity Revolutionizing Communication Systems in Smart Ports

The integration of technology and connectivity has brought about unparalleled advancements, creating efficient operations, improving safety, and enhancing the overall productivity of smart ports.

3.11.5.1 The Power of Seamless Connectivity

Seamless connectivity in smart ports refers to the ability to interconnect various devices, systems, and stakeholders with real-time data exchange.

By leveraging this technology, ports have been able to streamline their operations and improve communication among different entities involved in the logistics and supply chain process.

Some of the key features and advantages of seamless connectivity in smart ports include:

- ***Real-time data exchange:*** With seamless connectivity, smart ports can transmit real-time information about vessel arrivals and departures, container status, and other critical logistics data.

This ensures that all stakeholders are well-informed and can make informed decisions based on accurate information.

- ***Improved efficiency:*** By eliminating manual processes and enabling automated data exchange, seamless connectivity allows for improved efficiency in operations. This leads to faster turnaround times, reduced waiting times for vessels, and more efficient allocation of resources.
- ***Enhanced safety and security:*** Seamless connectivity enables smart ports to implement advanced security measures, such as video surveillance, access control systems, and real-time tracking of goods. This ensures a safe and secure environment for handling valuable cargo and mitigates the risk of theft or unauthorized access.
- ***Optimized resource allocation:*** Through seamless connectivity, smart ports can collect and analyse data from various systems to optimize the allocation of resources. This includes efficiently managing labour, equipment, and space, resulting in cost savings and increased productivity.

3.11.5.2 The Key Takeaways

The revolution in communication systems brought by seamless connectivity has had a profound impact on smart ports. To summarize, here are the key takeaways:

- Seamless connectivity enables real-time data exchange, improving the flow of information between stakeholders in smart ports.
- Smart ports leveraging seamless connectivity experience improved efficiency, enhanced safety, and optimized resource allocation, leading to cost savings and increased productivity.
- The global smart ports market is growing rapidly, with a projected value of $5.3 billion by 2025.

- The adoption of seamless connectivity in smart ports has the potential to generate significant value, estimated at $1.6 trillion over the next decade.
- The future of smart ports is inevitably tied to seamless connectivity, with the majority expected to embrace this technology by 2025.

Seamless connectivity has truly revolutionized communication systems in smart ports. By embracing this technology, ports can enhance their operations, increase efficiency, improve safety, and ultimately contribute to a more connected global supply chain. The future of smart ports lies in maximizing the potential of seamless connectivity and harnessing its power to create a more interconnected and efficient global logistics network.

3.12 Secure Communications

These technologies can be used for the migration of real time communication systems towards more advanced systems based on a distributed communication logic, using, for example, Machine-Type Communication (MTC) and particularly the IoT paradigm.

The command and control of the Autonomous Surface Vessels are based on reliable algorithms for autonomous navigation and guidance.

The use of these kinds of algorithms reduces the need for a human operator's interaction with the vessel and increases exponentially the amount of data exchanged between ships or between a vessel and the ACC.

In scenarios where the human component is limited to the control systems' detriment, MTCs are the most appropriate technological solution to support communications. Performing control through thousands of sensors disseminated within the vessel system, the IoT paradigm is the most appropriate to deploy network architectures suitable for different application scenarios for autonomous shipping, such as search and rescue, aids-to-navigation, and smart navigation.

From the examples of autonomous shipping presented, it is evident that the fundamental goal for network infrastructure is to provide reliable connectivity to heterogeneous types of systems and maritime applications and services, potentially based on the IoT communication paradigm.

The maritime scenario's challenges need to be addressed and modify the communication infrastructures accordingly to provide reliable network infrastructure.

The network infrastructure must provide ubiquitous connectivity between vessels and ashore stations, on a global scale, especially over open oceans, to ensure the unbroken and consistent existence of services, such as those based on AI algorithms used for the assisted navigation. Note that the ubiquitous connectivity needs of the roaming service among countries traversed by the vessels during navigation. In this scenario, the network infrastructure must be based on communication protocols that can convey nonuniform data traffic.

Indeed, marine traffic near the ports, shore stations, and waterways is very dense. On the contrary, marine traffic on the high seas, mainly generated by intercontinental transportation or blue water shipping, is relatively sparse in density. Due to maritime services' multiplicity, it is imperative to design the network infrastructure adopting a Service-oriented logic.

Maritime applications and services vary from simple periodic reporting to route exchange and remote control, such as in the autonomous shipping use case.

So, the communication infrastructure will be required to support a wide variety of maritime services, adapting itself to specific needs and match changing resource demands of those services.

Hence both network configuration and communication resources must be made flexible and adaptive to the offered service.

Further, the network needs to ensure that only qualified or authenticated services are available to the vessels or maritime devices, and vice versa, for maritime safety and security.

In addition to the multiplicity of services, the communication infrastructure must connect heterogeneous devices that range from the low-end or low-cost type with reduced functionality to the high-end type with advanced functionality.

Low-cost devices are adopted, for example, controlling the surroundings using low-power consumption devices, which generate a small amount of data.

The high-end devices are adopted onboard large vessels that encompass dense sensor networks, advanced navigation control systems, and navigation-support systems.

In this scenario of both heterogeneous application services and devices, maritime traffic can rapidly grow, as expected, with the diffusion of IoT-based services such as the remote command and control for autonomous ships or the AI algorithm for the assisted navigation.

Hence, the communication infrastructure must be designed considering both scalability needs in terms of bandwidth and computing resources, and capacity constraints due to the maritime hardware in terms of radio spectrum and bandwidth of the channels. So, the communication infrastructure must provide communication and computing support for heterogeneous devices and services.

For such a reason, the communication infrastructure must offer interoperability functionalities, i.e., the communication infrastructure must allow the data exchange and the integration of the information flexibly, effectively, consistently, and cooperatively.

Only guaranteeing the interoperability, it can be provided with access to the network for the different maritime applications and services, based on the IoT paradigm, seamlessly both within and across network boundaries, and provide portability of information efficiently and securely across the complete spectrum of maritime IoT services without effort from the end-user or host, regardless of its manufacturer or origin.

The allocation of the radio communication spectrum is the last challenge for the design of the communication infrastructure with a global coverage nature. Indeed, the radio spectrum is typically allocated opportunely by each nation following its regulations.

To successfully deploy a communication infrastructure worldwide and to function correctly, it is imperative that an international frequency band is available and established with appropriate international standards and regulations.

A communication infrastructure based on hardware components suitable for machine type traffic solves integration between the various types of devices and services relying on the IoT paradigm. Moreover, these technologies can allow the communication of thousands of devices, known as massive-MTC (mMTC)

Concerning the possibility of providing ubiquitous connectivity, the choice to exploit satellite technology offers several advantages: coverage over broad geographical areas, integration with the IoT paradigm. Finally, spectrum allocations for satellite communications in the maritime environment have been already defined.

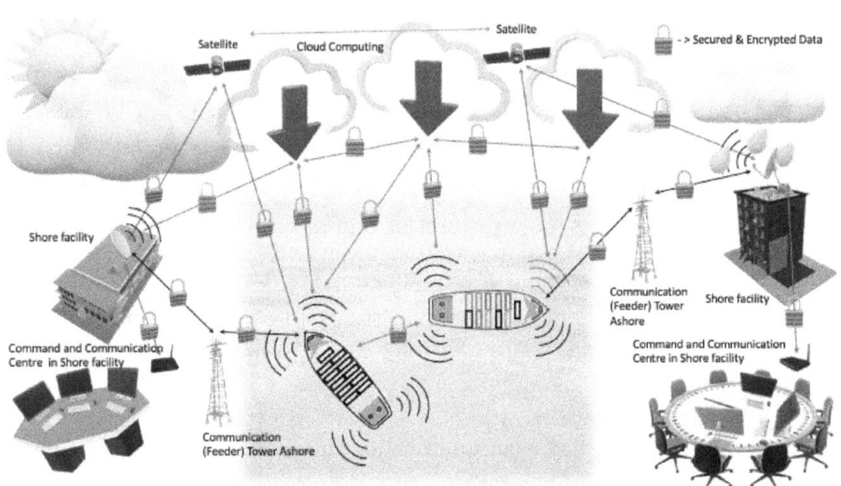

Ship to ship, ship to shore (to the command centre with the help of communication towers), ship to shore (via satellite to the command centre), intersatellite links and cloud services for ships and shore facilities.

Figure 3.7 - Example of Communication Infrastructure

Figure 3.7 is an example of deployment of a space-earth integrated maritime MTC infrastructure, based on the communication modes. A mobile station is an MTC terminal aboard a vessel or embedded in marine equipment in this infrastructure. It provides access to the infrastructure for marine equipment or an Ad-hoc network among vessels.

We can deploy the maritime cloud in the shore station, acting as a trusted platform to provide various maritime services and applications with the highest computational and storage capacity in the maritime IoT framework.

The functionalities for the management and orchestration of the communication infrastructure can run in the cloud.

Examples of these functionalities are the dynamic resource allocation, service resolution, and forwarding mechanisms; thus, the physical infrastructure resources can be maximally shared among service providers and are fine-tuned to meet the individual service requirements enabling service-centric networking. A dense network of shore control stations (near shore) can be deployed, allowing communication among the vessels in the shore and maritime clouds' proximity.

This kind of communication can generate more hyper-dense traffic than that originated during offshore communication. Note that vessels can achieve ad-hoc communications to facilitate direct communication among nearby mobile stations for maritime proximity services. In this infrastructure, the satellite can act in both ways providing access to the communication infrastructure or acting as a relay toward a shore station.

GEO satellite technology has shown some drawbacks compared to terrestrial radio ones, such as the inefficient covering of a high-dense traffic area due to its large footprint, high propagation delays, which affect both bandwidth management and congestion control algorithms, and error-prone links, which require forward error correction techniques to guarantee service reliability.

Notwithstanding, the new generation of LEO satellites offers a good alternative for maritime and IoT communications, as in the scenario considered in this work. LEO satellites have a propagation delay of about 10ms and a smaller footprint than geostationary satellites, so multiple satellites configured in constellations can be used to provide continuous coverage. Low Earth Orbit satellites have a circular (or elliptical) orbit at a height of 250 to 2000 km from the Earth's surface (Figure 14.3). The orbit period, mainly depending on the altitude, varies in the range 90 to 120 min. The satellites in the constellation communicate via inter-satellite links and toward the ground stations through feeder links.

Despite the reduced footprint and delay, LEO satellites can be yet unsuitable to serve areas with high-dense traffic, such as harbours and waterways.

In this case, a network of shore stations can allow partitioning the communication effort in the high-dense traffic areas, handling the communications coming from a cluster of vessels.

Furthermore, the shore stations can facilitate the optimised assignment of the satellite radio channels, increasing the communications infrastructure's capacity. In this scenario, tight interference management, i.e., intra-cell and inter-cell co-channel interference, is critical in achieving high spectral efficiency and system capacity in such dense deployment.

Note that the shore station could need centralised medium access control to reap the full benefit of the terrestrial communication infrastructure.

Table 3.1 shows the comparison of the communication technologies considered in this section starting from the existing literature. The first part of the table compares the various communication technologies regarding their ability to provide ship-to-ship (S-S) communication in an ad-hoc way or through ship-to-infrastructure (S-I), for the communication scenarios shown in the Figure 3.7.

The first part of the table shows the technology's ability to support communication near the coast or in the harbour (near-shore) or in the open sea (off-shore) where it is not possible to rely on any communication infrastructure. Note that, in the table both the WiFi and 4/5G technologies are evaluated, which offer ease of deployment of both ad-hoc and infrastructure-based communications networks. Both technologies provide data rate levels more than adequate for the applications considered in this paper, but the WiFi has the drawback of the poor communication ranges especially when obstacles are in the communication areas, such as in a harbour. Instead, 4/5G has the drawback that the communications always flow through the network infrastructures of the providers.

The last consideration should be made about the VDES technology widely used onboard the ships. VDES technology in both satellite (SAT) and terrestrial (TER) versions can provide data rates that are not exceptionally high. However, some studies considered in this section have highlighted the potential of this technology to be exploited for the transmission of information with data rates close to megahertz.

		Native				Non-Native		
		AIS	**SaT AIS**	**VD ES**	**SaT VDES**	**SatCom**	**WiFi**	**4/5G**
S-S	**Near-Shore**	No	Yes	Yes	No	No	Yes	Yes
	Off-shore	No	Yes	Yes	No	No	Yes/ No	Yes/N o
S-I	**Near-Shore**	Yes	Yes	Yes	Yes	Yes	Yes	Yes
	Off-shore	Yes	No	No	Yes	Yes	No	No
	MTC	Yes	Yes	Yes	Yes	Yes	Yes	Yes
	BC	No	No	Yes /No	Yes/ No	Yes	Yes	Yes

Table 3.1 - Native and Non-Native Maritime Communication Technologies vs. Communication Scenarios

In the second part of the table, the same technologies were compared in terms of their ability to support different levels of data traffic.

Precisely, we consider the medium / low levels of data traffic provided by the MTCs, such as that generated by small sensors and actuators of cyber-physical systems of the ship, up to high levels of traffic provided by the Broadband Communications (BC), such as that generated by applications that exploit the control logic based on AI algorithms or applications that exploit the logic of reality and augmented vision.

3.13 CSMA in Computer Networks

The following article is an extract from https://www.pynetlabs.com/csma-cd-vs-csma-ca/ with the kind permission of Mr. Devinder Thakran, PyNetLabs.com.

Quote

"CSMA stands for Carrier Sense Multiple Access; it is a protocol that helps transmit and reception data across a network. In order to ensure optimal transmission of data packets, it is necessary to minimize the possibility of packet loss and protect the integrity of the data on the network.

Without CSMA, each computer trying to transfer data must first find whether or not any other computers are actively sending data across the network. If the computer detects a transmission already in progress, it will wait its turn before sending it.

CSMA allows for simultaneous transmission and reception from several computers or nodes on a network. Each computer on a network receives the same data when one computer sends it out.

We now have a basic understanding of CSMA; let's move on to the CSMA CD and CSMA CA.

What is CSMA CD?

CSMA CD stands for Carrier Sense Multiple Access – Collison Detection. It is a media access control method used in Ethernet networks to ensure that only one device can transmit data on the network at a time.

When a device wants to send data, it first listens to the network to check if it is idle or busy. If the network is idle, the device can start transmitting else it waits.

How Does CSMA CD Work?

Only one network interface card (NIC) may transmit a frame in a single collision domain. However, the frame on the wire may be monitored simultaneously by all NICs. A NIC will check for the presence of other frames on the cable before sending its own.

If the wire is made of copper, the NIC can tell whether or not a frame is there simply by measuring the voltage across it. If it's an optical fiber cable, the detecting frame may be found by analysing the light frequencies on the cable. This whole process is known as carrier sense.

A NIC will wait for a frame to be sent if it finds one on the wire. When no other frame is present on the cable, a NIC will transmit the frame. It is possible for two or more NICs to simultaneously detect no frame. Consider the case when, for some reason, no frame is present on the wire, but two NICs are eager to send one. Due to the absence of a preceding frame, both NICs transmit their data packets simultaneously. This situation is known as multiple access.

A collision occurs when two or more NICs detect the cable at the same time but see no frame, and then both or all of them transmit their frames. Copper wire voltage and fiber optic light frequency are both affected in this situation. The situation is known as collision detection.

Let's take an example to understand how collision detection works.

As we can see from the following figure that there are 4 devices on a single collision domain. Device d1 is trying to transmit data to device d3. Device d2 is also trying to send data to device d3. As both devices, d1 and d2, send data at the same time; a collision will occur, as shown above. Now, the question arises what will happen after the collision? Let's understand.

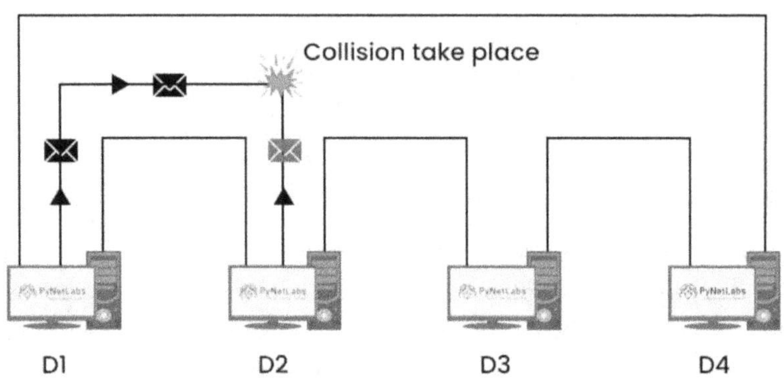

The NICs must resend the frames if they detect a collision for the frames they have sent. Each NIC that was sending a frame at the time of the collision sends out a unique signal on the network line known as a jam signal.

After a short amount of time, it re-senses the wire. In the absence of any more frames, the NIC will retransmit the one it originally sent.

A user would not be able to notice the microsecond-long delay caused by the NIC. The duration they wait is likewise random to ensure that a collision doesn't happen again when these NICs retransmit their frames.

More devices on an Ethernet segment mean more possibilities for collisions. If there are fewer nodes on the link, the throughput will improve as a result of collisions. As a result, keeping tabs on the frequency with which collisions occur throughout your whole network is essential. The throughput will decrease as the number of collisions increases.

We have already studied the working of CSMA CD; now let's discuss its advantages and disadvantages.

Advantages of CSMA CD

Some of the advantages of CSMA/CD are:

- It is simple and inexpensive to implement, as it does not require complex hardware or software.
- It is efficient and fair, as it allows every device to have an equal chance of transmitting data when the medium is free.
- It is robust and adaptable, as it can handle variable traffic and network conditions and recover from collisions quickly.

Disadvantages of CSMA CD

- The efficiency of CSMA CD decreases with distance, making it inappropriate for long-distance networks.
- The performance of collision detection is negatively impacted when a large number of devices are introduced to a Carrier Sense Multiple Access with Collision Detection (CSMA CD) system.

We have explained CSMA CD in detail; now, let's understand what CSMA CA is and how it works with its advantages and disadvantages.

What is CSMA CA?

CSMA CA stands for Carrier Sense Multiple Access – Collison Avoidance. It is a network protocol that operates in the data link layer of the OSI model. It uses carrier sensing to check if the channel is idle before transmitting data. It also uses collision avoidance techniques such as interframe spacing, contention windows, and acknowledgments to reduce the chances of collisions. CSMA/CA is mainly used in wireless networks, where collision detection is difficult or impossible.

How Does CSMA CA Work?

Wireless local area networks use a protocol called Carrier Sense, Multiple Access/Collision Avoidance (CSMA/CA). Collisions cannot be detected in wireless media as they can in Ethernet. In a WLAN, a device cannot simultaneously transmit or receive data. It either does one thing or it doesn't. As a result, it is unable to recognize when two frames collide.

Below we have shown a figure that helps you understand how it works:

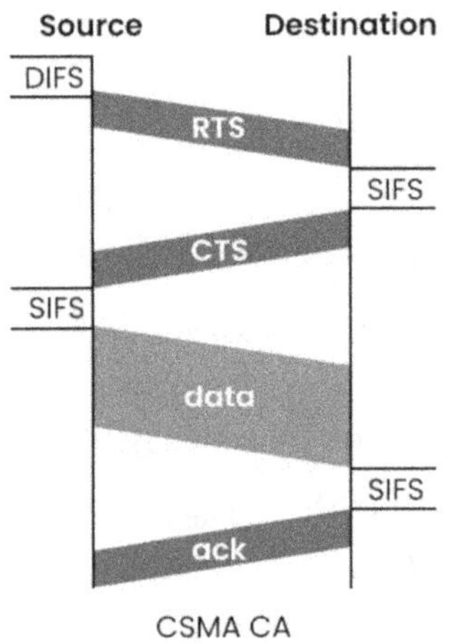

CSMA CA

To prevent a collision, devices rely on signals called "Ready to Send" (RTS) and "Clear to Send" (CTS). A device will scan the airwaves for a signal when it is ready to send. If there isn't already one, it will create a request to transmit (RTS) signal. It then delivers its own data and concludes with a CTS signal, which lets other wireless devices know it's their turn to communicate.

Advantages of CSMA CA

- When data packets are large in size, collisions are less likely to occur in CSMA CA.
- It takes care of the data packets and sends them off to their destination as necessary.
- Instead of detecting collisions on the shared channel, it is used to avoid them.
- CSMA CA ensures that no transmitted data is ever lost or wasted.
- The RTS/CTS extensions are used to cut down on unnecessary network traffic.

Disadvantages of CSMA CA

- Compared to CSMA CD, it is less effective.
- Each station utilizes a larger amount of bandwidth.
- On some occasions, the CSMA/CA protocol shows a delay that is double the duration of the average amount of time required to transmit a data packet.

Now, in detail, let's compare CSMA CD vs CSMA CA.

CSMA CD vs CSMA CA

Below we have explained the difference between the two in detail with some of the important factors.

Collison handling: The main difference between CSMA CD and CSMA CA is how they handle collisions. CSMA CD detects collisions after they occur and tries to recover from them. CSMA CA avoids collisions before they occur by using a handshake mechanism.

Network type: The network type that uses CSMA CD is Ethernet, which is a wired network. The network type that uses CSMA CA is wireless LAN (WLAN), which is a wireless network.

Efficiency: The efficiency of CSMA CD depends on the network load and the propagation delay. As the network load increases, the probability of collisions increases, reducing efficiency. As the propagation delay increases, the time to detect collisions increases, which also reduces the efficiency. The efficiency of CSMA CA depends on the network load and the overhead of RTS/CTS/ACK frames. As the network load increases, the contention probability increases, reducing efficiency. As the overhead of RTS/CTS/ACK frames increases, the time to transmit data decreases, which also reduces efficiency.

Data frame transmission: The data frame transmission in CSMA CD is binary exponential backoff, which means that after each collision, the device doubles its waiting time before trying again. The data frame transmission in CSMA CA is uniform backoff, which means that after each contention, the device chooses a random waiting time from a fixed range before trying again.

IEEE Standard: The IEEE standard that defines CSMA CD is 802.3, which is also known as Ethernet. The IEEE standard that defines CSMA CA is 802.11, which is also known as WLAN."

Unquote

3.14 Benefits of Autonomous Shipping

- Huge competitive advantage; ships' operations are already a combination of sea and shore-based roles.
- Higher earnings (reduced opex cost by about 22% at cruising speeds) thereby reducing cost of shipping cargo.
- Positive earnings already at lower freight rates

- Attractive payback; autonomy technology is progressing faster than anyone predicted.
- Reduced risk with more secure supply chains.
- Greater flexibility - adapt to market demand fluctuations.
- Significant emission reductions (up to 60%).
- Economic way to reach the IMO target of 50% CO_2 reductions.

3.15 Big Data Analytics in the Maritime Industry

3.15.1 Operations

- ✓ Maximises energy savings during operations.
- ✓ Safely guides vessels along routes
- ✓ Schedules management
- ✓ Usage of dashboards help to monitor information in real time.
- ✓ Reduces bunkering costs.

3.15.2 Technical Management of the vessel

- ✓ Safe operation of the vessel
- ✓ Real-time monitoring of the vessel's condition and maintenance activities
- ✓ Environmental protection regulations and governance
- ✓ Cleaning of components of the vessel such as the hull and propellers from barnacles, etc.

3.15.3 New Vessel Building

Design optimisation and improved hydrodynamics

3.15.4 Chartering

- ✓ Chartering involves finding the best value for money to deliver the cargo.
- ✓ BDA can assist in aggregation of information from a variety of sources such as Automatic Identification System (AIS), vessel characteristics such as maximum loading capacity, size, etc and other market insights on a single platform.
- ✓ Find alternatives if necessary.

3.15.5 Ports and Related Authorities

- ✓ Cargo handling operation / streamlining of the movement of goods.
- ✓ Timely maintenance of machinery such as cranes within the port
- ✓ Integrating services such as weather, to better safety and health concerns
- ✓ Better analysis of reefer containers for any potential or harmful health hazards.

3.15.6 Challenges in implementing BDA in the Maritime Industry

3.15.6.1 Increasing Cyber Threats

- × CPS and other cyber equipment are vulnerable to ever-increasing cyber-attacks.
- × Poor cyber security expertise within the maritime and related entities

3.15.6.2 Inaccurate Data Generated by Maritime Entities

Broadcasting fake call signs, inaccurately mentioning the next port of call, etc., will result in extremely incorrect analysis of information and lead to poor decision-making by the industry.

3.15.6.3 Other Challenges in the Industry Thar Precede over BDA Apps

Challenges such as labour shortages, over-supply and market fluctuation take precedence over BDA applications in the industry.

3.15.6.4 Lack of Shared Technology Implementation

Companies are focused on their functional silos rather than viewing the holistic picture and improving the entire maritime industry by using technological solutions.

3.15.6.5 Lack of Skills / Expertise

There is a dearth of data scientists to build BDA solutions.

3.16 Distributed Ledger Technology and Transparency

DLT is a de-centralised digital database of an auditable and immutable (unchanging) nature. Once information is altered, it is shared with all the nodes in the network, and it does not have a controlling / governing entity. A Smart Contract is a self-executing code which executes once a set of pre-determined conditions are satisfied like a contract. Smart Contracts can be used to check conditions when selling a ship, unloading cargo, etc. Assistance in reducing crime and fraud as traceability will help the regulatory bodies to identify and punish the relevant entities and personnel. It ensures that the health and safety standards for perishable items such as food in reefer containers are up to international standards.

3.17 Automation of Processes via Bots

Robotic Process Automation is used to automate repetitive and mundane tasks. It is a form of business process automation technology based on software robots or on artificial intelligence or digital workers. It is also known as software robotics or bots. It offers up to about 70% in cost reduction and 3x faster processing

Pre-automation implementation will require evaluation of all processes and standardising all the inputs, outputs, and the processes too. This will further enhance the efficiency of processes within the industry.

Bots can be used for a variety of tasks such as:

- Crew clearance – preparing the immigration and emigration documents.
- Informing ports and harbours about the arrivals and departures of vessels.
- Reading standard operating procedures of the industry
- Better compliance and governance within the industry to reduce fraud, malpractices, and corruption.
- Scheduling and tracking of shipments.
- Processing of invoices and collecting credit from vendors
- Monitoring and ensuring the maximum safe loads are carried in vessels
- Automated processing of shipping orders and shipment
- Automated email notifications to each stakeholder about the payments (when arrived / picked-up, etc)
- Automated processing of procurement and inventory management (etc ordering when minimum order quantity has been reached)
- Faster invoicing due to seamless integration between different portals of different entities
- Faster processing of claims and customer queries

3.18 Autonomous Ships' Endeavours Around the Globe

3.18.1 Remote Control

In August 2017, operations of an OSV sailing off the coast of Aberdeen were controlled remotely from San Diego, 8000 km away, using standard bandwidth (< 75 kb) onboard satellite communication. The retrofitting of the DP software was completed within just 30 hours. The benefits found were:

- Efficient use of resources,
- Least climate impact
- Highest safety

3.18.2 Rolls Royce and Finferries

Back in 2018, Rolls Royce partnered with Finland's government-owned ferry operator Finferries to create the world's first autonomous ferry. Falco - a car ferry navigated the waters without any human intervention during its journey from Parainen and Nauvoo, Finland. The Falco which comes with several advanced sensors could determine its surroundings with an unparalleled level of accuracy.

3.18.3 Navantia

A Spanish tech giant Navantia Sistemas came up with an aluminum autonomous ship that has been actively operating for the Port of Ceuta. Navantia created the boat called USV Vendaval in partnership with AISTER, a prominent player in the marine industry. The USV Vendaval can navigate autonomously and can even undertake activities like sea traffic control, surveillance, and castaway rescue missions.

3.18.4 Nippon Foundation

Nippon Foundation is working on the ambitious plan to automate up to 50% of Japan's local ships in the next twenty years. To this end, they have received the backing of Nippon Yusen the largest shipping company in the country.

To quote the General Manager of Nippon Yusen, "When it comes to the automation of ships, our mission is to have Japan lead the rest of the world. We need this technology to be recognized, otherwise, actual implementation in society will not move forward."

Nippon Foundation is undertaking the DFFAS (Designing the Future of Full Autonomous Ship) project. This project is a comprehensive system aimed to facilitate the operations of crewless autonomous vessels.

By February 2022 they are planning to run an automated container ship from Tokyo Bay to a coastal city called Ise. This 236-mile voyage will determine the efficacy of self-steering ships in an area with high marine traffic.

3.18.5 Yara

Norwegian fertilizer manufacturer Yara teamed up with tech company KONGSBERG to come up with the Yara Birkeland- the world's first fully autonomous, zero-emission cargo ship. Additionally, this vessel will lower the emission of CO_2 and Nitrogen Oxide, enhance road safety, and even lower sound pollution. Starting next year, this 87-yard vessel will replace truck haulage by 40,000 trips a year between Porsgrunn and Brevik. KONGSBERG will oversee all the technical aspects of this ship. This includes sensors, control systems, batteries etc. Last week, the Yara Birkeland made its maiden voyage in the Oslo fjord

The First Autonomous Battery-Powered 80 m, 120 TEU Container Vessel with zero emissions that Sailed in Norway

Figure 3.9 - Yara Birkeland

In the words of Svein Tore Holsether the CEO of Yara, "We are proud to be able to showcase the world's first fully electric and self-propelled container ship.

It will cut 1,000 tonnes of CO_2 and replace 40,000 trips by diesel-powered trucks a year." The Yara Birkeland is capable of loading and offloading the freight, navigate and recharge its batteries without any human intervention. Furthermore, the sensors will allow the ship to easily detect any object on its way so that it can avoid hitting anything.

To begin with, the ship will do two trips a week shipping 120 twenty-foot containers of fertilizers each time. "Now we have taken this technological leap to show it is possible, and I'm thinking there are so many routes in the world where it is possible to implement the same type of ship," adds Mr. Holsether.

2020	2025	2030	2035
Reduced crew with remote support and operation of certain functions	Remote controlled unmanned coastal vessel	Remotely controlled unmanned ocean-going ship	Autonomous unmanned ocean-going ship

Table 3.2 - Stages in Advancement Over the Next 10+ Years

***

O'REILLY
THE X TEAM
Guido van Rossum
Rheinwerk Computing
Learn Coding Fast
Matt Harrison
Nathan Hunter
SAP PRESS
ByteByteGo
JORGE BRASIL
sitepoint
The Pragmatic Engineer
Make: Community
IT REVOLUTION
RMC LEARNING SOLUTIONS
nigelpoulton
TOWARDS AI
Pragmatic Bookshelf

www.ingramcontent.com/pod-product-compliance
Lightning Source LLC
LaVergne TN
LVHW010115170826
845678LV00012B/2426

* 9 7 8 9 3 5 5 4 2 6 7 8 9 *